KS2 Science Revision

Jackie Clegg

Welcome to the magical world of Wizard Whimstaff – a wise wizard with great scientific powers!

Whimstaff wants to pass on his powers to you. He has some friends to help him.

Miss Snufflebeam – a forgetful young dragon who is always getting confused...

Pointy – Whimstaff's smart goblin assistant...

And Mugly and Bugly – Pointy's lazy pet frogs, who prefer eating and snoozing to learning, but still have a few tricks to teach you.

Just work your way through the pages of this book and you too will become a real Science wizard like Wizard Whimstaff and his friends!

Good luck, young wizard!

Contents

⭐ Humans

tick wh
complet

⭐ Plants

⭐ Animals and Habitats

Materials

Physical Processes

Food

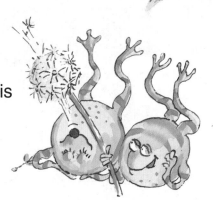

Burp! Food is yummy. Our favourite food is insects. What is your favourite food?

Different types of food.

Slurp! There are lots of different types of food. Let's put these foods into groups. Each food group does a different job in your body.

| These foods contain carbohydrates. | These foods contain protein. | These foods contain fats. |

We need foods to grow.

The insects we eat give us **protein**, so that we can grow. When you eat foods like meat and fish, the protein in these foods helps your body to grow bigger and stronger. Our woodland friend, the rabbit, does not eat meat. He likes to get his protein from plants like peas and beans.

People who do not eat meat are called vegetarians. They need to eat foods like cheese, nuts, peas and beans to get the protein they need.

We need foods to be active.

Slurp! Mugly and I have noticed that Pointy likes to move around a lot. We like to sleep a lot!

To move around, your body needs energy. This energy comes from **carbohydrates** in foods like pasta and potatoes.

Sugar and starch are the carbohydrates inside these foods. Carbohydrates provide your body with energy to run and play. You also get some energy from **fats**.

Healthy diet.

A healthy diet has some of each food group. Try to avoid eating too many foods that contain fats.

Brain cell alert! Do you have your '5 a day'? We should all eat 5 portions of fruit and vegetables every day.

Fruit and vegetables contain **fibre**. We all need fibre to help us **digest** our food.

 Did you know that 75% of your body is water? That's why it is important to drink lots of water.

MAGIC WORDS protein · carbohydrates · fats · fibre · digest

Wizard's Practice

Workbook page 4

Match up the foods with the job they do in the body by drawing a line.

1. bread and pasta   growth and repair

2. meat and cheese   energy to play and run

3. fruit and vegetables   extra energy

4. butter and crisps   help us to digest our food

Teeth

My teeth are all different shapes. So are Wizard Whimstaff's! Can you help me to find out more about teeth and why they are all different sizes?

 Different teeth.

Use a mirror to look at your teeth.

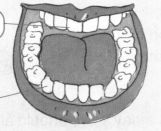 

incisors

canines

molars

Your front teeth are your **incisors**. These teeth are flat with a sharp cutting edge. Use your tongue to feel the shape of your incisors. Next to your incisors are the cone shaped teeth. They are called **canines**. Now move your tongue to your back teeth. These teeth are wider and flatter on the top. They are called **molars**.

 Keeping teeth healthy.

There are bacteria in our mouths. The bacteria feed on the sugars left on your teeth and make a sticky substance called **plaque**. This causes our teeth to decay. To keep our teeth and gums healthy we need to:

Brush our teeth twice a day.

Visit the dentist twice a year.

Use dental floss and mouthwash.

Avoid eating too many sugary foods.

It is important to look after your adult teeth because no more will grow through after these. So if your tooth is rotten and has to be removed, you will be left with a space.

Different teeth for different functions!

Pointy says that the different shaped teeth do different jobs.

This is an incisor.

The incisors chop your food into small pieces.

Sheep and cows have well developed incisors to help them eat grass.

This is a canine tooth.

The canine teeth tear food.

Lions and tigers have well developed canines to help them tear at their prey's flesh.

This is a molar tooth

The molars chew and grind food.

You have lots of molars to chew your food.

MAGIC WORDS   incisor · canine · molar · plaque

Workbook
page 5

Wizard's Practice

Can you help me to finish these sentences?

1. My front teeth are called _____ .

2. I chew food with my _____ .

3. To keep my teeth healthy, I should not eat too many

_____ .

4. To keep my teeth healthy, I need to visit the _____

5. Lions and tigers have well developed _____ .

Skeleton and movement

Your skeleton is made up of hundreds of bones. Without it, you wouldn't be able to move. Let's look at the bones inside your body. Can you name some of them?

Skeletons

You have a **skeleton** inside your body, just like me. Your skeleton supports and protects your body and holds you upright. Your skeleton grows with you. As your skeleton grows larger, so do you. Super! Look at the different parts of the skeleton.

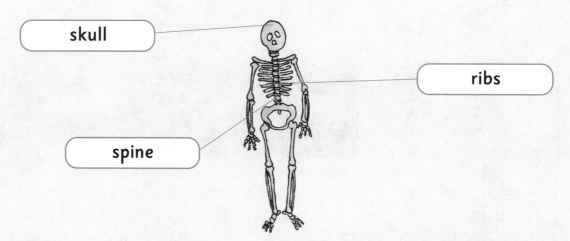

skull

ribs

spine

Not all animals (yes, humans are classed as animals!) have their skeletons inside their bodies.

Animals such as insects and crabs all have their skeleton on the outside of their bodies. Look at these pictures.

An insect skeleton is on the outside. It cannot grow like an internal skeleton, so in order to grow bigger, the insect has to shed its skeleton and grow a new one.

Bones

Your bones are hard and very strong. The surface of your bones is also very smooth, so it does not damage any organs or muscles.

Unfortunately, if you have a bad fall, bones can break. Look at this X-ray of a leg bone. If you look carefully, you will see that the middle of the bone is hollow.

 If our bones were solid, they would be very heavy and it would be difficult for us to move around.

Muscles and movement.

Bones do not bend. We can only bend where two or more bones meet. This is called a joint. Muscles are attached to bones. To move the bone, the muscle contracts or shortens, which pulls the bone in one direction.

bicep contracts and pulls up lower arm

triceps muscle relaxes

Muscles can only pull, they cannot push. When a muscle has pulled a bone into a new position, it cannot push it back. Another muscle contracts to pull it back.

This is why muscles always work in pairs. It's easy when you know how!

 The more exercise we do, the harder our muscles work. When our muscles work hard, we start to feel hot and tired.

MAGIC WORDS skeleton · joint · muscle

Workbook page 6

Wizard's Practice

Now answer these questions by filling in the missing spaces.

1. My skeleton _____ my body and holds me upright.

2. My bones are made of a material that is hard, smooth and _____.

3. Insects and crabs have skeletons on the _____ of their bodies.

4. Bones move when they are pulled by _____ .

5. Muscles always work in _____ .

Heart and blood

Allakazan! I need to tell you about one of the most important organs inside your body… your heart! Without your heart, you wouldn't stay alive!

Your heart!

Your **heart** is about the size of your clenched fist.

Your heart is in the centre of your chest. It is protected by your ribs.

Your heart is made up of muscles. The muscles contract to squeeze **blood** out of the heart.

Hey presto! Your heart pumps blood to all parts of your body.

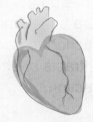

Your heart beats as it pumps blood out and round the body.

Blood vessels.

Let me tell you how your blood travels through your body.

Your blood is moving around your body all of the time. It travels through small tubes called **blood vessels**.

The blood vessels that carry blood away from your heart are called **arteries**. After your blood has moved all around your body, it travels back to the heart in **veins**.

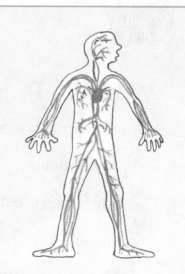

Your heart starts to pump blood around your body before you are born and carries on non-stop for the rest of your life.

Your pulse.

When your heart pumps, the blood is forced through your arteries. This causes a ripple along your arteries.

When your arteries are close to the surface of your skin you can feel this ripple. Allakazan! This is your **pulse**.

You can feel for your pulse and count the number of ripples in one minute. This is called your pulse rate.

When you run and jump, your muscles work harder.

When your muscles work harder, they need a greater supply of blood.

To provide more blood, the heart needs to pump faster.

Your heart beat increases, so your pulse rate increases.

When you are resting, your pulse rate is about 70 beats per minute.

MAGIC WORDS

heart · blood · blood vessels
arteries · veins · pulse

Wizard's Practice

Workbook page 7

Now try these by ticking the correct box.

 1 The heart is protected by the: skull ☐ ribs ☐ hips ☐

2 Blood is carried away from the heart in:

arteries ☐ tubes ☐ veins ☐

3 When you exercise, your pulse rate:

stays the same ☐ decreases ☐ increases ☐

 4 At rest your pulse rate is about:

7 beats per minute ☐ 70 beats per minute ☐

70 beats per second ☐

Growing up

You are growing up! Soon you will become a teenager and after that you will become an adult. Super!

 Life cycle.

When you were a baby, your parents did everything for you. They gave you food and drink, and kept you clean and warm.

As humans grow through their **life cycle**, they depend on their parents less. Although children start off very small, they still look similar to their parents.

Life cycle of a human

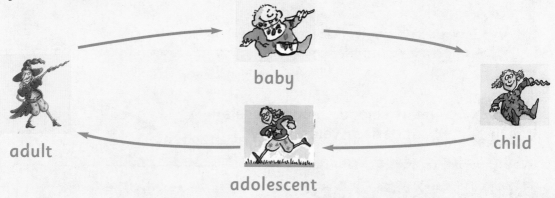

When Mugly and Bugly were first born, they did not look anything like their parents. They started off as frog spawn and developed into tadpoles, before finally changing into frogs.

Life cycle of a frog

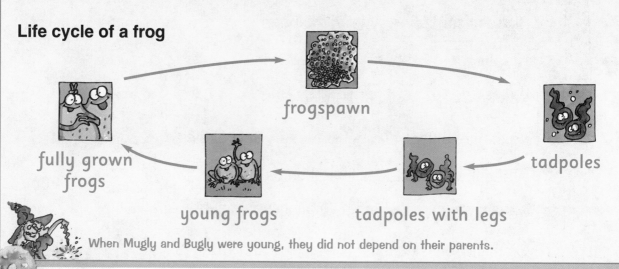

When Mugly and Bugly were young, they did not depend on their parents.

Being healthy.

There are lots of things you can do to stay healthy. You need a healthy diet. This means eating some food from each of the food groups. Don't forget your '5 a day' and drink lots of water.

You need to exercise to stay healthy. The more you exercise, the more your blood moves around your body. This is good for your heart and the rest of your body.

Sometimes when you are ill, the doctor will give you medicine. This is a drug that will help you to feel better. Your doctor tells you how much medicine to take and when you need to take it. If you take too much of your medicine it could be harmful.

 It is important to keep medicines out of reach of small children.

Being unhealthy.

Some adults drink alcohol. Drinking a small amount of alcohol is fine when you are grown up. However, drinking too much damages the body. You may have seen some adults smoking. When people smoke, it causes damage to their body, which can even kill them.

Some people choose to take tablets that are not medicines. These tablets affect the way their body works. We call these tablets drugs. People that take drugs cause a lot of damage to their minds and bodies.

 MAGIC WORDS life cycle

Workbook page 8

Wizard's Practice

Write **T** next to the true sentences and **F** next to the false sentences.

1. You grow through different stages. This is called a life cycle. _____

2. To stay healthy, you should do very little exercise. _____

3. A healthy diet includes lots of chips. _____

4. Your doctor will tell you how much medicine to take. _____

5. Smoking, drinking too much alcohol and taking drugs are all harmful. _____

Wizard's Challenge

 Food

Croak! Have a go at these while we have a snooze. Here are some types of food.

group 1  group 2 group 3

a Which group of food are carbohydrates?   group _____

Explain why a runner should eat lots of carbohydrates before a race.

_____

_____

b Which group of food should you eat 5 times a day?   group _____

Explain why you should have '5 a day' of these foods.

_____

_____

 Teeth

Brain cell alert! Answer these questions.

a Which type of teeth are used for grinding food? _____

b Write down two things that you should do to help keep your teeth healthy.

1 _____

2 _____

3 Skeleton and movement.

a Label these bones. Choose your answers from this list: backbone, ribs, skull.

[ ]

[ ]

[ ]

b Which part of the skeleton protects the brain? _____

c Describe how muscles move our bones.

_____

_____

4 Heart and blood.

a Describe what a runner's heart does during a race.

_____

b Describe the difference in his pulse after the race.

_____

5 Growing up.

Burp! Tick the activities that give you a healthy lifestyle.

eat lots of chips [ ]   take plenty of exercise [ ]

play computer games [ ]   smoke cigarettes [ ]

drink lots of water [ ]   eat a balanced diet [ ]

Growing plants

We don't eat plants, but you do! Humans grow plants especially to eat.

Plants for food.

Farmers and gardeners grow lots of plants for you to eat. You eat different parts of the plants.

part of the plant	what we eat	
leaves	lettuce, cabbage	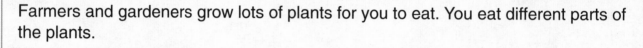
roots	carrots, parsnips	
fruit and seeds	tomatoes, peas, sweetcorn, apples	
flowers	cauliflower, broccoli	
stem	celery	

Germination

Seeds are the start of the plant life cycle. We have some seeds that we are going to grow into plants. First of all, the seeds will develop into tiny plants. This is called **germination**.

For the seeds to germinate they need air, warmth and some water. Then the plants will grow bigger. That's when you eat them!

 Too much water stops the seeds germinating and air reaching the seeds.

Plants need water!

The plants in the garden take some of the water from our pond. They suck the water up through their roots. Slurp!

The water passes up through the stem to all of the other parts of the plant.

Some of the water goes into the leaves, which is where plants make their food. Water is needed for plants to make their food.

Croak! Watering plants is an important job. You need to give them the right amount of water.

Plants that do not have enough water start to **wilt**.
Plants that are overwatered will soon die.

 A slug ate all the leaves on our plant. This stopped the plant from growing.

MAGIC WORDS germination · wilt

Wizard's Practice

Workbook page 9

Brain cell alert! Finish these sentences.

1. For seeds to germinate they need air, _____ and some _____ .

2. Plants make their food in their _____ .

3. Plants take in water through their _____ .

4. When seeds develop into tiny plants, it is called _____ .

5. If a plant does not have enough water, it will start to _____ .

Plants make their own food

Plants need food so that they can grow taller and produce more leaves and flowers. Just like you need food so that you can grow!

⭐ Plants need light!

Let's see what happens if you leave a plant in the dark for a week.

When we look at the plant after it has spent a week in the dark, it has thin, yellow leaves. If you leave a plant in the dark for much longer, it will eventually die.

Put the plant in the sunlight and its leaves will soon turn green again!

There is a green chemical inside the plant that absorbs the sunlight. The sunlight provides the energy for the plant to make its food. Allakazan!

Plants produce their own food so we call them producers.

18

Making food.

The more food plants can make, the more they can grow. Plants living in a greenhouse grow faster than the plants left outside in the garden.

This is because the greenhouse is warm. The warmth allows the plant to make food faster.

The greenhouse also allows lots of light to reach the plants. The more light that shines on the plant, the more food it can make.

Hey presto! To make their food, plants take in air through their leaves. They also need water, which they take in through their roots.

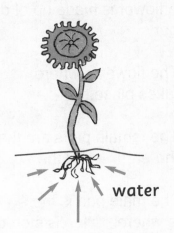

The air and water combine together, using the energy from sunlight, to produce food. The food passes from the leaves to all parts of the plant so that new growth can take place.

water

The roots also anchor the plant into the ground.

 MAGIC WORDS producer

Workbook page 10

Wizard's Practice

Finish the sentences.

1. Plants make their own food in their _____ .

2. Plants combine air and _____ to make their food.

3. Plants get their energy from _____ to make their own food.

4. Plants produce their own food, so we call them _____ .

5. Plants that have been left in the dark have thin, yellow _____ .

The flowering plant

I like flowers, but it can be hard to remember what all of the different parts are called. Wizard Whimstaff has made a diagram to help me.

 ## Parts of the plant.

A flower is made up of different parts.

The flower is where **reproduction** takes place.

The female parts are the **ovary**, the **stigma** and the **style**.

The male part is the **stamen**. This is where **pollen** is stored.

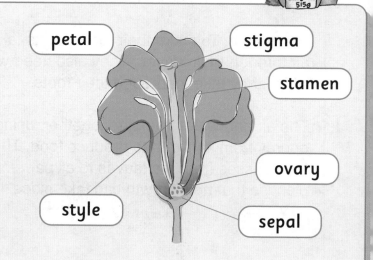

petal | stigma | stamen | ovary | style | sepal

You can remember that the stamen is the male part of the flower because it has the word 'men' in its name.

 ## Fertilisation

Can you work out what happens during **fertilisation**? Pollen is carried to the flower. The pollen grains become stuck on the sticky surface of the stigma. Then the pollen travels down the style into the ovary. Once inside the ovary, the pollen grain fuses with an **ovum**. This is called fertilisation. After fertilisation, the seeds start to form.

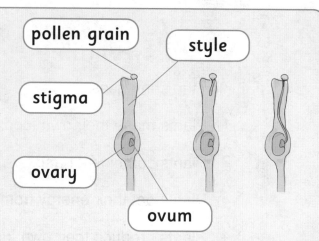

pollen grain | style | stigma | ovary | ovum

The seeds are surrounded by a store of food. This is called the fruit. We can eat the fruit of some plants.

Different jobs.

Do you know which job each part of the flower does?

part of the flower	job it does
petals	Attract insects to the flower.
sepal	Protects the flower while it is in bud.
stamen	The male part of the flower that stores pollen.
stigma	This is the sticky surface which pollen becomes stuck to.
style	The tube that connects the stigma to the ovary.
ovary	The female part of the flower where the ovum is stored.

This picture shows the female part of the flower.

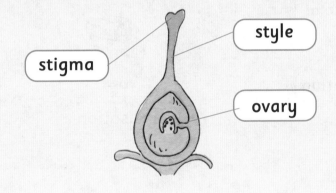

Insects or wind can carry pollen from one flower to the stigma of a different flower.

MAGIC WORDS reproduction · ovary · stigma · style
stamen · pollen · fertilisation · ovum

Workbook page 11

Wizard's Practice

Can you match each word with its meaning?

1 fertilisation   male part of the flower that stores pollen

2 stamen   the part where reproduction takes place

3 flower   when the pollen grain fuses with the egg

4 ovary   formed after fertilisation, will develop into new plants

5 seeds   female part of the flower where the ovum is stored

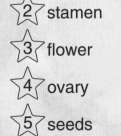

Life cycle of plants

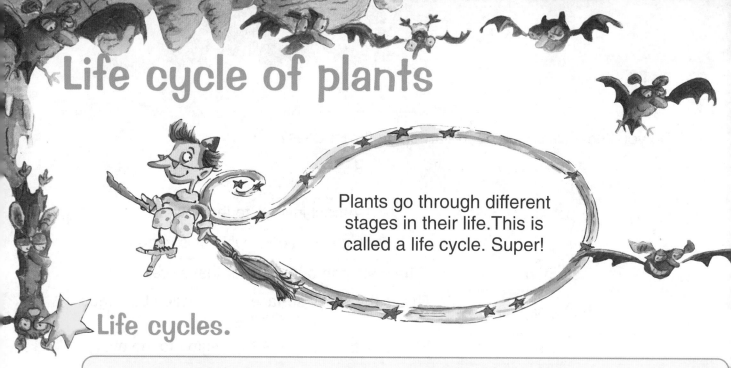

Plants go through different stages in their life. This is called a life cycle. Super!

⭐ Life cycles.

Plants start their life as seeds. After germination the tiny plants will start to look like their parent plants.

seed dispersal → germination → growth → pollination → fertilisation → seed formation → seed dispersal

During your life cycle you will look similar to your parents. This is different for plants and some animals.

⭐ Pollination

Pollen is stored in the tip of the stamen.

Pollen is carried from one flower to another by wind or by insects. This is called **pollination**.

The pollen grain lands on the sticky surface of the stigma. Part of the pollen grain moves down through the style and into the ovary. Inside the ovary, the pollen fuses with the egg. This is called **fertilisation**.

This is the start of a seed. It's easy when you know how!

Flowers that are pollinated by insects have coloured petals and a scent to attract the insects.

Seed dispersal.

When the seeds have developed, they fall to the ground and start to germinate. If the seeds fall to the ground under their parent plant, more new plants will be in competition with the parent plant for light, water and space.

The seeds need to move away from the parent plant. This is called **seed dispersal**. Seeds can be dispersed by different methods.

wind dispersal

animal or bird dispersal

explosion dispersal

water dispersal

MAGIC WORDS pollen · pollination · fertilisation · seed dispersal

Wizard's Practice

Workbook page 12

1. The process of carrying seeds away from their parent plant is called

   _____ .

2. When the pollen grain fuses with the egg, it is called _____ .

3. Pollen can be carried from one flower to another by either

   _____ or _____ .

4. Plants and animals compete with each other for resources such as

   space, _____ and _____ .

5. After fertilisation, _____ are formed.

Wizard's Challenge

1 Growing plants.

Wizard Whimstaff carries out an investigation to see if temperature affects how seeds germinate. He puts cotton wool into three identical tubs and adds 30 seeds. He leaves the tubs at different temperatures and waters the seeds regularly. Here are his results.

place	temperature of place	number of germinated seeds		
		day 2	day 4	day 6
fridge	cold	0	0	0
garden	cool	0	10	22
kitchen	warm	0	28	45

a Which factor did Wizard Whimstaff change? _____

b Write down **two** factors he kept the same.

1 _____ 2 _____

c Explain why it is important to change only one factor in an investigation.

_____

d Write a conclusion for this investigation.

_____

2 Plants make their own food.

a Circle the **three** things plants need to make their food. Time for a snack!

air   dark   fibre   light   vitamins   water

b Circle the part of the plant where they make their own food.

flower   leaf   root   stem

3 The flowering plant.

a Burp! Try to label the diagram of a flower whilst we have a snooze. Choose your words from this list:

ovary   petal   sepal   stamen   stigma   style

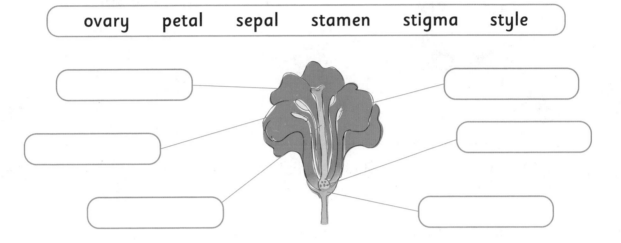

b In which part of the flower is pollen stored? _____

c Which part protects the flower when it is in bud? _____

4 Life cycle of plants.

a Slurp! Finish labelling the diagram of the life cycle of a plant. Choose your words from this list: wilting, pollination, seed dispersal, seedlings.

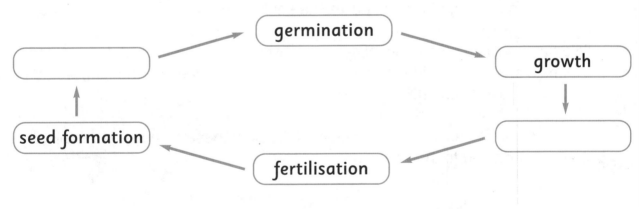

b Describe what is meant by **germination**.

_____

_____

Habitats

We like our habitat. It is where we live and where we catch our food. Grub's up!

⭐ Habitats

Burp! A **habitat** is a place where animals and plants live. Our habitat is the garden pond.

Other examples of habitats are woodland, seashore, river, desert and mountains.

Have you been to any of these habitats? Or perhaps you have read about them in adventure stories!

⭐ Animals in their habitats.

There are lots of things for us to eat in our habitat. We like to eat insects and slugs. Slurp! Our habitat is nice and moist. We need this so we can breathe. As well as food and moisture, our habitat gives us shelter and protection from other animals.

We have noticed that the local cat does not like our pond, which is handy for us! Animals are **adapted** to their own habitat. Our pond friends, the fish, would not be happy living in a desert!

You can match animals to their habitats. Look at these animals and think about how they are adapted to their habitat.

 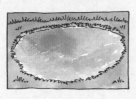  

Animals are part of the **community** of a habitat. The community is all of the living things in a habitat.

Plants in their habitats.

Brain cell alert! Plants are also part of the community in a habitat. Plants are adapted to their habitat.

Some seaweed has pockets of air trapped in the leaves. This means it can float near the surface of the water and absorb sunlight.

Plants growing in shady places often grow large, flat leaves. This allows them to absorb more sunlight in their shady habitat.

Cactus plants live in the desert. Their habitat has lots of sunlight and is very hot. Their leaves have adapted into tiny spines. Plants lose water through their leaves, so the spines reduce the amount of water lost by the cactus.

 An ecosystem is a habitat and its community.

MAGIC WORDS   habitat · adapted · community · ecosystem

Workbook page 13

Wizard's Practice

Write **True** or **False** next to each sentence.

1. The habitat for a fish is the desert. _____

2. An oak tree is part of the community of a forest. _____

3. Animals do not form part of a community. _____

4. The habitat for a camel is the polar ice cap. _____

5. Plants and animals are adapted to their habitat. _____

Identification

Now we are going to look at how we can place animals and plants into different groups to help us to identify them. Hey presto!

Using a Venn diagram.

Animals and plants have different **features**, such as shape of leaf, number of legs, wings or no wings. We can group things according to their features. We use a **Venn diagram** to help us sort things into different groups. Each circle contains animals or plants with the same features. You place animals or plants that have features from both circles into the middle section where the circles overlap.

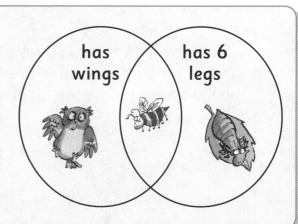

Using a key.

Looking at the features of animals and plants can help us to identify them. One way of doing this is to use a classification key. Each part of the key asks a different question about their features.

Use this key to identify these animals. You need to look at each animal and work through the key for it.

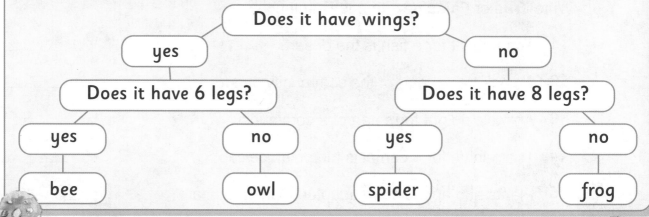

Does it have wings?

yes — no

Does it have 6 legs?   **Does it have 8 legs?**

yes — no   yes — no

bee — owl   spider — frog

Grouping plants and animals.

Let's look at how we group plants and animals. When grouping animals, the first feature we look for is a backbone. The backbone is actually made up of lots of small bones, called vertebrae. Animals with backbones are called vertebrates and this group includes cats, dogs and horses. Humans have backbones so we are vertebrates too, as are fish, birds and snakes. Animals without backbones are called invertebrates. Some examples of invertebrates are insects, worms and shellfish.

We can group plants by those that produce flowers and those that do not produce flowers.

flowering plants   non-flowering plants

 Everyone in the world uses the same features to group plants and animals. This means we all know what type of plant or animal we are talking about.

 MAGIC WORDS   features · Venn diagram
vertebrates · invertebrates

Workbook page 14

Wizard's Practice

Can you match each word with its meaning?

1. invertebrates   parts of an animal or plant used to identify them

2. vertebrates   animals without backbones

3. features   animals with backbones

4. classification key   a way of sorting animals and plants into groups

5. Venn diagram   a method of identifying animals and plants

Food chains

Croak! We like food chains. They are just a way of showing who eats what!

Producers

Burp! **Food chains** start with green plants. The green plants produce their own food, so we call them **producers**.

Plants use energy from sunlight to make their own food. This food energy is then passed along the food chain.

The Sun provides energy for the food chain.

Food chains.

Croak! There are rose bushes in our garden. Greenfly feed on the rose bushes. Ladybirds eat the greenfly. This is a food chain. The arrow means 'is eaten by'.

rosebush   greenfly   ladybird

The greenfly and ladybird are called consumers. In the food chain below, the lettuce plants are the producers. We are consumers and so are the slugs. Time for a snack!

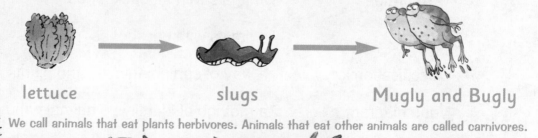

lettuce   slugs   Mugly and Bugly

We call animals that eat plants herbivores. Animals that eat other animals are called carnivores.

Food webs.

Herbivores usually eat more than one type of plant. **Carnivores** often eat more than one type of animal. This means food chains become linked together. When food chains link together, we call them **food webs**. Slurp! Can you find one food chain in this food web?

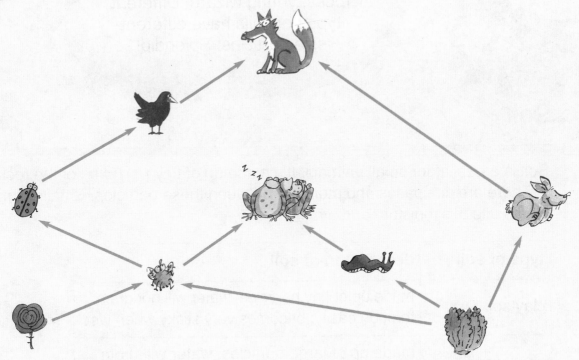

Parts of the food web are connected. When one part changes, it will affect other parts of the food web. For example, when the gardener picks all of the lettuce, there will be fewer slugs. So we will have fewer slugs to eat! Then we will need to eat more greenfly.

MAGIC WORDS food chain · producer · herbivore · carnivore · food web

Wizard's Practice

Workbook page 15

Write **T** for True or **F** for False next to each sentence about the food web.

1. The lettuce is a producer. _____

2. The fox is a herbivore. _____

3. If the rose bush dies, Mugly and Bugly will need to eat more slugs. _____

4. The fox is eaten by the rabbit. _____

5. Mugly and Bugly are consumers. _____

Soil and rocks

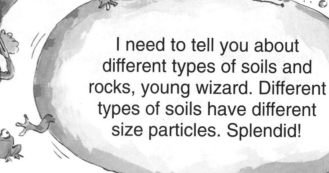

I need to tell you about different types of soils and rocks, young wizard. Different types of soils have different size particles. Splendid!

⭐ Soil

Soil is a habitat for small animals. It's made up of tiny **particles** of the rocks below it. There are air spaces and moisture between these particles. Small animals and plants use this moisture and air.

type of soil	description of soil
clay soil	made up of tiny particles; water will not drain through easily; becomes very sticky when wet
chalky soil	made up of large particles; water will drain through easily; pale, poor quality soil
sandy soil	made up of large particles; water will drain through easily; pale colour

⭐ Rocks

Rocks are found everywhere. We can find them lying on the ground, or as hills and cliffs. Rocks are grouped according to how hard they are.

We can use rocks to build houses, bridges, walls and statues.

Granite is very hard and is often used for buildings.

Chalk is very soft and can be used to make cement.

Hey presto! One way of testing the hardness of a rock is to try scratching its surface. A plastic knife will scratch chalk. An iron nail will scratch chalk and marble, but not granite.

Fertiliser

Gardeners put fertiliser on to the soil. The fertiliser can be animal droppings or chemicals. The fertiliser is dug into the soil where it breaks down into simpler chemicals called **nutrients**. These nutrients dissolve in the water in the soil. When the plant takes in water through its roots, it also takes in the nutrients. Allakazan!

Plants need nutrients for healthy growth.

Sometimes chemical fertiliser is advertised as plant food. This is not correct. Plants make their own food. The chemical fertiliser contains nutrients to help the plant grow stronger.

MAGIC WORDS   particles · nutrients

Wizard's Practice

Workbook page 16

Finish these sentences.

⭐1 Clay soil is made up of tiny _____ .

⭐2 Soil is made up of particles from _____ that are found below the surface of the ground.

⭐3 Plants and small animals use the moisture and air trapped in the

_____ .

⭐4 Farmers and gardeners improve the quality of their soil by adding

_____ .

⭐5 Fertilisers break down in the soil to form _____ for plants.

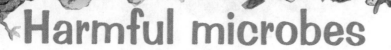

Harmful microbes

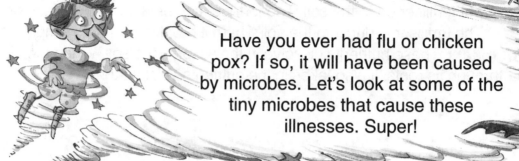

Have you ever had flu or chicken pox? If so, it will have been caused by microbes. Let's look at some of the tiny microbes that cause these illnesses. Super!

Microbes can cause illness!

Microbe is a short word for **micro-organism**. Micro means very small. Organism means a living thing. So a micro-organism is a very small, living thing. Micro-organisms are so small you need a microscope to see them. **Bacteria**, **viruses** and some **fungi** are micro-organisms. You'll soon get the hang of it!

Bacteria can cause illnesses such as food poisoning and ear infections.

Viruses can cause illnesses such as flu and measles.

Fungi can cause skin diseases such as athlete's foot.

We know micro-organisms are living things because they show all seven life processes. All living things (animals and plants) carry out seven life processes.

Moving   Reproduction   Sensitivity (or feeling)   Growth

Respiration (taking in air and using it to make energy)   Excretion (going to the toilet)   Nutrition (using food in your body)

 An easy way to remember all seven life processes is to take the first letter of each process. This spells Mrs Gren.

Microbes can cause food to decay.

The mould on bread is fungi. It feeds on the bread and grows on its surface. Food that is left in the air, and kept warm and moist, will allow millions of microbes to grow. We can preserve food by preventing microbes getting to it. There are a number of methods of preservation:

Sealing in packets to stop air reaching the meat.

Freezing to stop any microbes reproducing.

Heating to destroy microbes, then sealing in a tin to stop air getting in.

Microbes cause tooth decay!

Bacteria live in your mouth. The bacteria feed on the sugary foods that stick to your teeth. As the bacteria feed, they produce **plaque**. This plaque attacks your teeth and causes tooth decay. To prevent tooth decay you need to:

Brush your teeth twice a day.   Use mouthwash and dental floss.

Visit your dentist every 6 months.   Not eat too many sweets.

MAGIC WORDS   micro-organism · bacteria
virus · fungi · Mrs Gren · plaque

Workbook page 17

Wizard's Practice

Finish the sentences.

1. Micro-organisms include _____ , viruses and some _____ .

2. We know that microbes are living things because they carry out all seven _____ .

3. Bacteria can cause illnesses such as _____ and _____ .

4. Food decays because of _____ .

5. Bacteria in your mouth feed on sugar and produce _____ , which rots your teeth.

Helpful microbes

You've already looked at harmful microbes, but not all microbes are bad. Now we are going to see how useful some microbes can be. Splendid!

Microbes in food production.

Microbes are used in the making of food and drink.

Yeast is used to make bread, wine and beer.
Bacteria are used to make yoghurt and cheese.

Special microbes are added as the food or drink is being produced. When the microbes are added, the food is kept warm for a short while. This allows the microbes to reproduce.

When the process of making the food is finished, the food is kept cool to stop the microbes reproducing any more.

Decay

Microbes break down waste materials. The microbes grow on the materials and then feed on them. This causes the materials to **decay**. Hey presto! It is very helpful that microbes break down dead plants and animals. Microbes are used to break down the human waste that passes through our bodies.

Not all materials can be broken down. Materials like leaves, grass and paper decay easily, but plastic and glass do not decay. So you must recycle them.

Glass, metal cans and plastic bags can all be recycled.

The conditions microbes need to grow.

Microbes need air, water, food and warmth to grow and reproduce. Without any of these conditions, microbes cannot live.

Alexander Fleming was a famous scientist who lived from 1881 to 1955. He discovered a useful mould called penicillin.

Alexander Fleming was growing bacteria in dishes. He left the dishes by an open window. Some of the special mould blew in through the window and landed on the dishes. A few days later, Fleming was about to throw the dishes away when he noticed that the bacteria around the mould had started to die. The special mould had destroyed the bacteria. Allakazan! Penicillin is still used today to treat bacterial infections.

MAGIC WORDS   yeast · decay

Workbook page 18

Wizard's Practice

Circle the correct answer.

1. Yeast is used to make (soap   **bread**   crisps).

2. A material that decays is (glass   plastic   **paper**).

3. A condition needed for microbes to grow is (**warmth**   light   quiet).

4. When materials break down, it is called (delay   **decay**   deflate).

5. Alexander Fleming discovered (**penicillin**   medicine   mould).

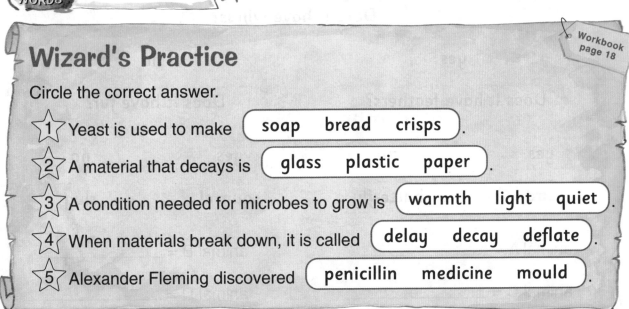

Wizard's Challenge

1 Habitats

a Croak! Draw lines to match each animal with its habitat.

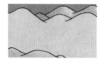

b Describe what is meant by the word habitat.

_____

2 Identification

a Slurp! Use the key to identify garden animals.

A   B   C   D

Does it have wings?

yes   no

Does it have feathers?   Does it have fur?

yes   no   yes   no

bird   butterfly   squirrel   slug

animal A = _____   animal B = _____

animal C = _____   animal D = _____

3 Food chains.

a Burp! In our garden, the rabbits eat grass and the fox eats rabbits. Show this information as a food chain. Write in the words to show each stage of the food chain.

[   ] → [   ] → [   ]

b Describe what would happen to the food chain if the fox died.

_____

4 Soil and rocks.

Pointy carried out an investigation into different types of soils.

Pointy added 20 cm^3 of water to each soil sample.

a Which soil sample was sandy soil and which was clay soil? Write A or B in the correct box.

sandy soil [   ]   clay soil [   ]

       A   B

b Give a reason for your answer.

_____

_____

5 Microbes

Some microbes can be used to make food and drink.

a Name a food or drink made using microbes.

_____

b Which type of microbe causes illnesses such as flu?

_____

Properties of materials

Look around your classroom or home. The room and all of the things in it are made up of different materials. All objects are made up of materials and there are lots of different ones.

⭐ Different materials for different objects.

Slurp! Think of an object, young wizard. It is made up of a **material**. Look at the materials below.

object	material
door	wood
window	glass
wall	bricks
hat	wool

⭐ Properties of different materials.

Now we are going to look at the **properties** of different materials. Different materials have different properties. When an object is made, the material is decided upon by its properties. The properties of the material need to match its use. A window made of bricks would not be very useful. A television cannot be made of paper!

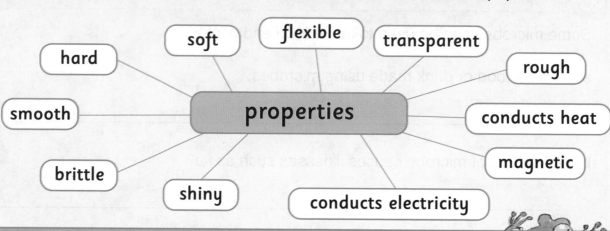

hard — soft — flexible — transparent — rough — smooth — **properties** — conducts heat — magnetic — brittle — shiny — conducts electricity

Fair testing.

We are going to carry out an **investigation** to see which paper towel will soak up the most water.

We need to make sure we carry out a **fair test**, so we will only change one **factor**. It is important to keep all of the other factors the same. If you change more than one factor, you will not know which factor caused your results.

We will change the type of paper towel.

We need to keep all of the other factors the same:

Volume of water.

Length of time.

Size of paper towel.

Size of bowl for water.

Balance used to weigh towel before and after soaking in water.

Now, when we have our results, we will know that it is the type of paper towel that causes the difference.

 Another word for a factor is a variable. These are the things you can change in your investigation.

MAGIC WORDS material · properties
investigation · fair test · factor

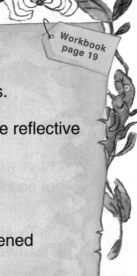

Workbook page 19

Wizard's Practice

Match each object to the material with the most suitable properties.

1. window   material that can be polished and made reflective

2. mirror   material that is soft and insulates heat

3. saucepan   material that is transparent

4. coat   material that is hard and can be sharpened

5. knife   material that conducts heat

Solids and liquids

I am not sure which things from my shopping basket are solids and which are liquids. Let's learn some rules so that I can group the rest of my shopping.

⭐ Solids

Oh dear, I know that my wooden spoon is a **solid** and my shampoo is a **liquid**. But what makes them a solid or a liquid?

Solids:

Don't change shape when you move them.

Do not flow, so you cannot spill them.

Might be able to conduct heat.

Might be able to conduct electricity.

Could be magnetic.

What about my spoons? They keep their shape. They can conduct heat and electricity. They are not magnetic. Abracadada! My spoons are solid.

The particles inside the solids are held firmly together. This is what gives solids their properties.

Pouring solids.

I have just poured sugar into my tea cup. I think sugar is a solid, but according to my rules solids cannot be poured.

Pointy says the sugar is made up of small, solid grains. This means it can flow.

Liquids

Oh dear. I used to think that all liquids were water. Then Pointy explained to me that lots of things can be liquid, not just water. What I need is a set of rules for the liquids. This will help me to sort the liquids from the solids.

Liquids:

Flow easily.

Can be poured from one container into another.

Take on the shape of the container they are in.

Always stay level on their surface.

Are never magnetic.

Do not conduct heat easily.

Do not conduct electricity easily.

What about my shampoo? It flows easily as it is poured from the bottle. It takes on the shape of the bottle and has a level surface. My shampoo is a liquid.

The particles inside liquids are not held firmly in place, so they can move around. This is why liquids have different properties from solids.

 MAGIC WORDS solid · liquid

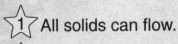 Workbook page 20

Wizard's Practice

Write either **True** or **False** next to each sentence.

1. All solids can flow. _____

2. All liquids can flow. _____

3. Most solids are rigid and keep their shape. _____

4. Solids can never conduct electricity. _____

5. Liquids take on the shape of their container. _____

43

Gases

We have gases all around us. We cannot see them, but we know they are there. Super!

Air is all around us!

We are surrounded by air all of the time. Air is a mixture of different types of gases. We cannot see the gases in the air, but we can see the effects of these gases.

We can see the effects of gases when we use air to blow up balloons, bicycle tyres and inflatable boats.

Air has a mass, which is the amount of material in a substance. Let me show you how I know. A balloon with air inside has a greater mass than an empty balloon. It's easy when you know how!

When I squeeze my sponge in my bath water, air bubbles rise to the surface. This is because air is trapped inside the sponge.

Properties of gases.

Gases are materials like solids and liquids, but they have some different properties.

Gases:

Can flow more easily than liquids.

Can be squashed into a smaller space.

Do not keep their shape.

Do not keep their volume

Spread out in all directions.

Can fill the container they are in.

The particles inside gases are not held in position, so they can move freely. This is why gases have different properties from solids and liquids.

Different gases.

There are lots of different gases and we can use most of them.

We use natural gas in our homes for central heating and gas cookers.

Carbon dioxide gas is used in fire extinguishers and to make drinks fizzy.

We use oxygen in our bodies. The oxygen from the air combines with the food we eat to give us energy.

Special gases are used in hospitals to put people to sleep before an operation.

Helium gas is put into party balloons to make them rise.

 MAGIC WORDS gas · properties · carbon dioxide · oxygen

Workbook page 21

Wizard's Practice

Match the magic word to its correct description.

1	air	a gas used inside balloons to make them rise
2	carbon dioxide	the gas I breathe in and use inside my body
3	helium	a mixture of gases that is all around us
4	oxygen	has mass, can flow easily and fills a container
5	properties of air	a gas used to make drinks fizzy

45

Changing state

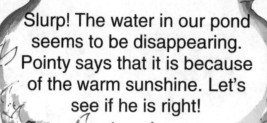

Slurp! The water in our pond seems to be disappearing. Pointy says that it is because of the warm sunshine. Let's see if he is right!

Changes

Croak! The water in our pond is a liquid. On very hot days, some of the water changes into a gas, which then mixes with the air. This is called **evaporation**. This means our friends have less water to play in.

On very cold days, our pond water freezes. It changes into a solid and ice forms on the surface of our pond. When the Sun comes out, the ice melts and becomes water again.

Pointy says that when water freezes to become ice, or when it evaporates to become a gas, it is changing state.

Drying out.

Water is evaporating all of the time, but we cannot see it. Sometimes evaporation is useful, like when wet clothes are hung out to dry. Pointy says warm and windy conditions are the best for drying clothes. Evaporation happens quickly in these conditions.

Other examples of evaporation are when you dry your hair with a hair dryer and when puddles dry up.

We can smell Miss Snufflebeam's perfume when the liquid evaporates and the gases reach our noses.

The water cycle.

Brain cell alert! We don't mind too much when the water evaporates from our pond, because when it rains it fills the pond up again. I wonder if it is the same water?

The **water cycle** shows how water changes state.

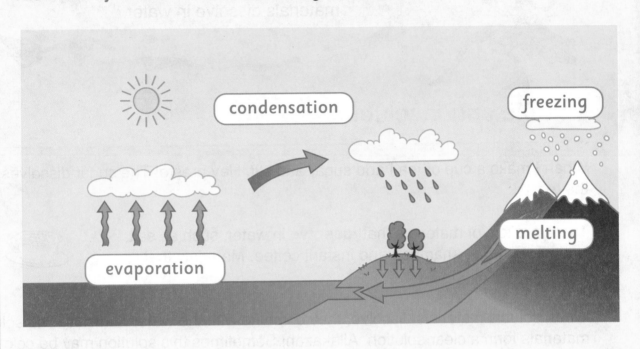

condensation

freezing

evaporation

melting

Water falls back to ground either as a liquid (rain) or a solid (snow).

Workbook page 22

MAGIC WORDS

evaporation · water cycle
condensation · melting · freezing

Wizard's Practice

Finish these sentences by writing the correct word in the space.

1 When a liquid changes into a gas, the name of the process is

_____ .

2 When a gas changes into a liquid, the name of the process is

_____ .

3 Freezing is when a liquid changes into a _____ .

4 Melting is when a solid changes into a _____ .

5 The _____ shows how water changes state.

Dissolving

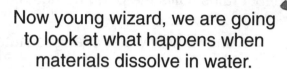

Now young wizard, we are going to look at what happens when materials dissolve in water.

Soluble and insoluble!

When I make a cup of tea I add sugar and stir. Hey presto! The sugar dissolves into the tea.

There are lots of materials that **dissolve** in water, such as salt, washing powder, shampoo and instant coffee. Materials that dissolve are called **soluble**.

When soluble materials dissolve, they combine with the water particles. The soluble materials form a clear solution. Allakazan! Sometimes this solution may be coloured but it is still clear.

Some materials, such as sand and chalk, cannot dissolve. These materials are called **insoluble**. When insoluble materials are added to water they can still be seen.

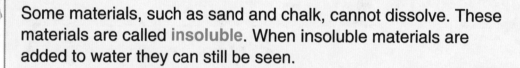

I can get my dissolved materials back. All I need to do is evaporate the solution to remove the water. The solid particles will be left behind in the dish.

Saturation

If you keep adding soluble materials to water, eventually no more will dissolve. All of the spaces between the water particles have become full. This means no more solid can combine with the liquid.

Hey presto! We have a **saturated solution**.

You can filter this mixture to remove the excess material that did not dissolve. You will be left with a clear solution.

Speeding up dissolving.

Let me tell you about how we can speed up dissolving. Pointy and I were in the kitchen making some jelly. We had a race to see who could dissolve their jelly faster and I won!

I got my jelly to dissolve more quickly by:

Using warmer water.

Cutting the jelly into smaller pieces.

Stirring.

Using more water.

The trouble is, I don't know which one of these factors contributed the most to the jelly dissolving. I changed too many factors all at once, so this was not a fair test.

Some materials are more soluble than others.

MAGIC WORDS dissolve · soluble · insoluble · saturated solution

Workbook page 23

Wizard's Practice

Write **True** or **False** next to each sentence.

 1. Sugar is insoluble. _____

 2. Sand is soluble. _____

3. You can speed up dissolving if you use warmer water. _____

4. When soluble materials dissolve, they combine with the water particles. _____

5. A saturated solution will allow more material to dissolve. _____

49

Separating mixtures

Separating mixtures is easy when you know how. You have to think about the properties of the materials. Then it is easy to think of a way to separate them. Super!

Magnetism

Wizard Whimstaff made a mistake and dropped all of his iron nails into a box of aluminium bolts.

I remembered that iron is **magnetic** and I helped him to separate them.

I used Wizard Whimstaff's magnet to pick out all of the iron nails.

You'll soon get the hang of it!

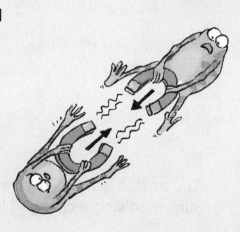

Sieving

Sieves can have different size holes to suit the job they have to do.

A gardener uses a sieve to separate stones from soil. The stones are too large to pass through the holes in the sieve, but the particles of soil are small enough to fit through.

A fisherman uses a net to catch fish from the sea. Mugly and Bugly use a net to catch yummy flies!

Sieves and nets can be used to separate solids from liquids.

Filtering

Wizard Whimstaff and I tried to clean a dish of water from Mugly and Bugly's pond. We tried using a sieve but the small soil particles just passed through the holes in the sieve, because the holes were too large.

Then we tried filter paper and a filter funnel. The small soil particles could not pass through the tiny holes in the filter paper. They were trapped on the filter paper. **Filtering** can be used to separate smaller solid particles from a liquid.

 A mixture of soluble and insoluble solids can be separated by filtering.

Evaporating

When we had filtered the dish of pond water it was clear. I thought it was pure water, but Wizard Whimstaff said that we needed to check to see if there were any soluble materials dissolved in it. So we **evaporated** the water. It's easy when you know how!

To do this we heated the pond water. As the pond water heated, **water vapour** (steam) rose from the water. All of the water evaporated and there were solid materials left in the bottom of the dish.

Workbook page 24

Wizard's Practice

Circle the correct word.

1. To separate iron coins from copper coins you could use
   filtering   sieving   magnetism .

2. To separate sugar from cornflakes you could use
   filter paper   a sieve   a magnet .

3. To separate sand from water you could use
   filter paper   a sieve   a magnet .

Reversible changes

Now young wizard, we are going to look at how materials can change state. Splendid!

Changing temperature.

Miss Snufflebeam's ice lolly has melted. This is called a **reversible** change because we can change it back. We will put the ice lolly in the freezer and it will turn back into a solid.

One cold night I left my drink of orange juice outside. Next morning my drink had frozen. This is a reversible change. I can warm my drink up and it will change back into a liquid.

I have boiled some water in the kettle. The steam has gone all over the window. The steam changes back into a liquid (condenses) as it touches the cool window. This is a reversible change.

Changes of state can be reversible.

Distillation

Let me tell you about **distillation**. I use this to separate a mixture of ink and water. As the mixture is heated, some of the water turns into water vapour. This is called **evaporation**.

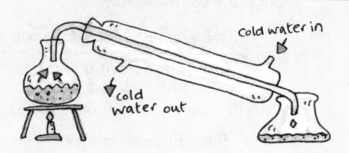

As the water vapour moves down the tube it cools and turns back into a liquid. This is called **condensation**. Pure water comes out of the tube and the ink powder is left behind in the beaker.

Making mixtures.

Miss Snufflebeam has mixed sand and water together.

> Pointy can separate it using filter paper. This is a reversible change.

Mugly and Bugly have mixed salt and sand together.

> I have added water to the mixture so that the salt will dissolve. Now I can filter the mixture to remove the sand. I evaporate the solution to remove the water and I am left with salt. This is another reversible change.

Most mixtures can be separated easily – they are reversible changes.

MAGIC WORDS   reversible · distillation · evaporation · condensation

Workbook page 25

Wizard's Practice

Use the magic words to finish the sentences.

☆1 When an ice cube melts, it is called a _____ change.

☆2 We can use _____ to separate a mixture of two liquids.

☆3 Two processes are involved in distillation. These are
_____ and _____ .

☆4 When salt is added to water, it will _____ .

☆5 A mixture of sand and water is a reversible change because we can
_____ the sand.

Irreversible changes

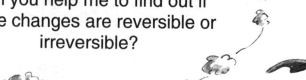

I always seem to be causing changes with my puffs of fire! Can you help me to find out if these changes are reversible or irreversible?

Cooking

Some materials change when they are heated up. When I fry my eggs, I cannot put them back to how they were at the start. Pointy says that this is an **irreversible** change.

The same happens when I bake bread or a cake. This must be an irreversible change because I cannot put them back to how they were at the start. Irreversible changes often make new and useful materials.

Burning

Sometimes my fire puffs get me into trouble, because I burn things by accident! One day I burnt Wizard Whimstaff's page of spells. It turned into smoke and ashes and I couldn't get the page back. Wizard Whimstaff said that this was an irreversible change.

Abracadada! Bonfire night is a wonderful time. I would like to put the fireworks back to how they were at the start, so that I could watch them all again. Pointy says that this cannot happen, because it is another irreversible change.

Burning causes irreversible changes. The wood on the bonfire changes to ashes and smoke. When I am cooking in the kitchen, I burn natural gas, which changes into different gases.

Wizard Whimstaff makes sure that we stay well away from things that are burning. You can injure yourself if you get too close.

When some materials burn, they give off harmful fumes.

Mixing

Some materials change when you mix them together.

You can see changes happening when you mix baking powder with vinegar. You can see bubbles forming. This shows that an irreversible change is taking place.

When I mix Plaster of Paris and water, they become warm and then form a hard solid. This cannot be changed back into powder and water, so I know that it is an irreversible change.

 If the materials cannot be put back to how they were at the start, the change is irreversible.

Workbook page 26

Wizard's Practice

Write **R** for Reversible or **I** for Irreversible next to each type of change.

1. Freezing water to make ice cubes.   _____

2. Mixing cement powder and water to make a hard solid.   _____

3. Melting butter.   _____

4. Burning a match.   _____

5. Dissolving salt into water.   _____

Temperature change

Let's have a look at **temperature** change and see how we can measure it. Using a thermometer or a data logger are just two different ways of measuring temperature. You'll soon get the hang of it!

★ Recording temperature.

When I touch Mugly and Bugly, they feel cool. When I touch my woolly scarf, it feels warm. The words **cool** and **warm** are not a very accurate way to record temperature. For an accurate measure of temperature, I need to use a thermometer.

Some important temperatures include:

Temperature of melting ice = 0°C

Average room temperature = 20°C

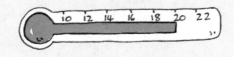

Body temperature = 37°C

Boiling point of water = 100°C

The symbol °C stands for degrees Celsius. We use a capital C because this is named after a scientist. If I need to be very accurate when measuring temperature, I can use a data logger and temperature probes. The temperature readings can be stored in the data logger. Super!

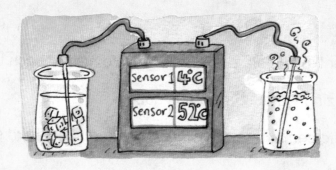

Temperature is a measure of how hot or how cold things are.

Keeping your drink cool.

When I am sitting in the garden, I enjoy a cool drink.

There are different ways of keeping my drink cool. I could keep my drink in the shade. I could add ice cubes to my drink. I could wrap a towel around my glass. The towel will act as an **insulator** and keep the cool in and the warmth out. The towel is a poor conductor of heat.

Thermos flasks can keep cool drinks cool or warm drinks warm. They are good insulators.

Thermal conductors.

When I make drinking chocolate, I heat milk up in a saucepan. My saucepan is made of metal.

The metal conducts the heat to the milk, so it can warm up quickly. Metal is a good **thermal conductor**. The saucepan handle is made of wood. This does not conduct heat. This stops me burning myself.

Saucepan handles are made of thermal insulators, as they do not let heat pass through.

  MAGIC WORDS   temperature · insulator · thermal conductor

Workbook page 27

Wizard's Practice

Match the key word to its correct meaning by drawing a line.

1	thermometer	material that will not allow heat to flow through
2	temperature	material that allows heat to flow through easily
3	insulator	an instrument to measure temperature
4	thermal conductor	a measure of how hot or how cold something is
5	degrees Celcius	unit of temperature

Keeping warm

Croak! In the summer, you can sit in the sunshine to keep warm. In the winter, when it's cold, you need a coat. Let's find out how a coat keeps you warm.

⭐ Thermal insulators.

Slurp! Air is a good insulator, so it does not allow heat to pass through easily. Materials that have air trapped inside them are good thermal insulators. A coat with a fluffy lining, a duvet and a woolly hat are all good **thermal insulators**.

Food from a take-away is served in polystyrene containers. Polystyrene is made from compressed foam, which has air bubbles trapped inside. The air insulates the food and keeps it warm. Thermal insulators can also be used to keep things cool.

Good thermal insulators keep cold objects cold and warm objects warm.

⭐ Fair testing.

Burp! We have been given lots of different materials. We want to investigate which material is the best thermal insulator. In order to make this a **fair test**, we can only change the type of material. If we change lots of **factors** we cannot be sure if it is the material that is affecting the temperature. We will wrap different materials around some beakers. We then pour warm water in the beakers and record the temperature change and how quickly each cools down.

We need to keep all other factors the same, such as:

Size of the beaker.

Volume of the water.

Starting temperature of the water.

Time beakers are left for.

Number of layers of insulating material.

Lids on all beakers.

Not stirring the water.

Results and conclusions.

We took the temperature readings of each beaker every two minutes for ten minutes. Then we wrote our results into a results table.

time	temperature (in °C)			
(in minutes)	cotton wool	towel	paper	plastic
0	50	50	50	50
2	46	45	47	46
4	42	40	39	37
6	38	34	31	29
8	33	31	26	24
10	32	28	22	20

Pointy says that a **conclusion** is what we have found out from our investigation.

We think that cotton wool is the best insulator because it kept the most heat in. So this is our conclusion.

Is it time for a snooze yet?

 Results tables always need headings at the top of the columns. Don't forget to add the units!

Workbook page 28

Wizard's Practice

Write **True** or **False** next to each sentence.

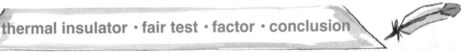

1 Thermal insulators allow heat to pass through them easily. _____

2 Air is a good insulator. _____

3 Thermal insulators can keep cool things cool. _____

4 A conclusion describes what you did. _____

5 In a fair test, you only change one factor. _____

59

Wizard's Challenge

 1 Properties of materials.

> Slurp! Pointy is warming milk for our drinking chocolate. The saucepan is made of metal. Which property of metal makes it useful as a saucepan? Circle one box.
>
> conducts electricity   shiny   conducts heat   cold

 2 Solids, liquids and gases.

> Burp! The diagram shows our bottle of pop. Label the diagram. Choose your words from **gas**, **liquid** and **solid**.

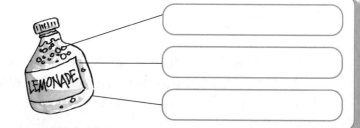

 3 Separating mixtures.

> Croak! Pointy is separating a mixture of pebbles, sand and salt. The picture shows some of the things that he could use.
>
> **a** What should Pointy use to separate the pebbles from the mixture?
>
> _____
>
> **b** Pointy wants to separate the sand and the salt. Describe how Pointy could separate this mixture.
>
> _____
>
> _____

4 Reversible changes.

We put some ice cubes into different places. We timed how many minutes it took for each ice cube to melt. Here are our results.

place	garden in sunlight	garden shed	under the tree	Pointy's bedroom
time taken to melt in mins	30	45	40	20

a Draw a bar chart of our results.

b Which place was the warmest?

_____

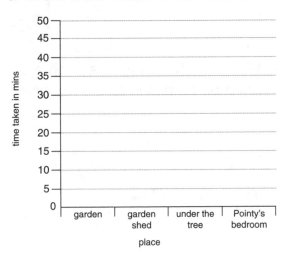

5 Keeping warm.

Slurp! We like our coffee warm. We are carrying out an investigation to see which cup will keep our coffee the warmest.

a Write down one thing we need to keep the same to make this a fair test.

_____

_____

b Write a conclusion for our experiment.

_____

_____

Magnets

Magnetism is a type of force. Forces act between magnets. One end of the magnet will always point north. We call this end of the magnet the north pole. We call the other end the south pole. Super!

⭐ Attract and repel.

When you put two magnets near to each other, sometimes they move together. We call this attraction.

When the two magnets push away from each other, this is called repulsion.

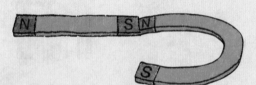

Opposite poles attract and like poles repel. It's easy when you know how!

 Magnets show attraction to other metals, but repulsion is the true test to show if something is a magnet.

⭐ Useful magnets.

Magnets are used at the recycling centre. They sort out the metal cans.

Cans made of iron are attracted to the magnet.

Aluminium cans are not attracted to the magnet.

Magnets can be used on cupboard doors to help them stay closed.

Magnets are also used inside the loudspeakers of music systems.

Magnetic and non-magnetic.

Some metals are attracted to a magnet, so we call these metals magnetic.
Some metals are not attracted to a magnet, so we call these metals non-magnetic.

Iron and nickel are magnetic. Some metal alloys are magnetic. An alloy is a material that is made up of a mixture of metals. Alloys containing iron or nickel are magnetic. Steel is an alloy that contains iron, so steel is magnetic too.

I used a magnet to find out which items are magnetic and which are non-magnetic. Here is a table of my results.

Some metals that are non-magnetic are aluminium, silver, lead, zinc and tin.

magnetic	non-magnetic
iron nail	plastic bottle
iron filings	kitchen foil
paper clip	wood
metal can	copper pipe
key	gold ring

Some metals make stronger magnets than others.

MAGIC WORDS   magnetic

Wizard's Practice

Workbook page 29

Write **A** when there will be attraction.
Write **R** when there will be repulsion.
Write **N** when nothing will happen.

1. north pole and north pole _____

2. south pole and north pole _____

3. south pole and south pole _____

4. bar magnet and a silver ear ring _____

5. horse shoe magnet and paper clips _____

Seeing the light

Light is very important. In order to see anything, we have to have light. Allakazan!

Sources of light.

Let me tell you about light sources, young wizard. Light travels from a light source.

Examples of light sources include the Sun, an electric lamp, a candle and a torch.

If you are not sure if an object is a light source, try to imagine the object in a dark room. Only a light source will give out light. Allakazan!

A mirror is not a light source, because it doesn't give out light. A mirror only reflects light.

 Anything that gives out light is a light source.

Reflecting light.

When light hits a smooth surface it bounces off. The light is reflected. Smooth, shiny surfaces reflect light very well. Objects that are good reflectors of light include: shiny metal foil, glass, glitter, the moon. The ray diagram shows how Miss Snufflebeam can see her reflection in the mirror.

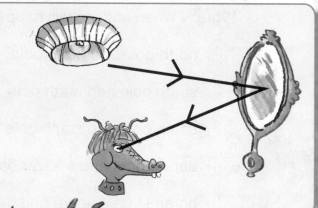

Ray diagrams.

Have you ever wondered why you can't see around corners? It is very simple. Light can only travel in straight lines. Light travels from a light source into your eyes. We see things because light bounces off them. Splendid!

Light travels from the light source, which is the torch.

It bounces off Miss Snufflebeam's head.

It then travels into my eye. This means that I can see Miss Snufflebeam's head.

To draw a ray diagram you need to:

Use a ruler to draw a straight line.

Draw a continuous line, without any breaks.

Show the direction the light is travelling in by adding arrow heads to the lines.

Check that you have drawn the light travelling into the eyes.

Light does not travel from our eyes, it always travels into our eyes.

 MAGIC WORDS 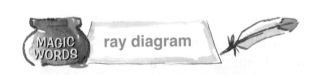 ray diagram

Workbook page 30

Wizard's Practice

Underline the correct word.

1. Light travels in   wavy lines   curved lines   straight lines.

2. When light bounces off an object, this is called

    reflection   refraction   radiation.

3. A drawing showing the direction of light is called a

    light path   ray diagram   picture diagram.

4. Which of the following will reflect light the best?   soil   brick   metal foil.

5. An example of a light source is   the Sun   a mirror   a window.

Shadows

Can you help me to understand shadows? Pointy says that a shadow from an object or person forms an outline, but has no detail or colour.

Making shadows.

I have noticed that not all objects form shadows. Pointy says that only objects made from opaque materials will form a shadow. Opaque materials block the light, and when light is blocked, a shadow forms.

Some materials let light pass through them, so they do not form a shadow. These materials are transparent.

 Reflections are different from shadows. Reflections show detail and colour.

The Sun.

I have just found out that my shadow changes. At different times of the day, my shadow can be a different size and point in a different direction.

I thought it changed because the Sun moves across the sky, but Pointy says that the Sun doesn't move. He says that actually the Earth rotates, which makes it appear as if the Sun is moving across the sky.

sunset   midday   sunrise

My shadow will be longer in the morning and the evening when the Sun is low in the sky.

My shadow is shortest at midday, when the Sun is directly over my head.

Investigating shadows.

I want to investigate the size of shadows. I think that the size of the shadow changes as it moves closer to the light source.

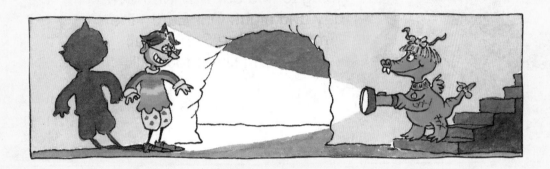

Pointy says that I must make this a **fair test**. This means I can only change one **factor**. I will change the distance Pointy stands from the torch.

Factors I will keep the same are:

The size of the torch.

The position of the torch.

Pointy.

The position of the wall.

I found that the closer Pointy is to the torch, the larger his shadow is.

MAGIC WORDS   fair test · factor

Wizard's Practice

Workbook page 31

Write **T** for True or **F** for False at the end of each sentence.

1. Shadows form when light is blocked. _____

2. Transparent materials form shadows. _____

3. Opaque materials block light. _____

4. The Sun moves and the Earth stays still. _____

5. Shadows are longest early in the morning and late in the evening, when the Sun is low in the sky. _____

Earth, Sun and moon

Now young wizard, we are going to find out why we have day and night. Our Earth, the moon and the Sun are all **spherical**, like a football.

Our Earth!

The Earth, Sun and moon are too big for us to look at properly, so we can use models. We can use a football for the Sun, a tennis ball for the Earth and a pea for the moon.

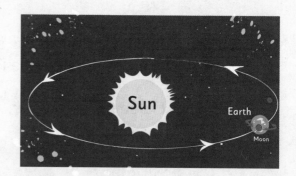

The Sun is a huge star, it gives out light. All of the planets in our solar system orbit the Sun.

It takes one year (365 days) for Earth to orbit the Sun. Allakazan!

Our Earth is a planet, so it does not give out light. Only stars give out light.

Day and night.

The Earth is spinning all of the time. We call this rotation. It is the Earth's rotation that gives us day and night. Hey presto!

When our side of the Earth is facing the Sun, we have daytime. When our side of the Earth is facing away from the Sun, we have night-time.

It takes 24 hours for the Earth to rotate once.

The rotation of the Earth gives the impression that the Sun is moving across the sky.

Changing moon.

Now young wizard, have you noticed how the moon appears to change shape from one night to the next?

The moon orbits the Earth. It takes 28 days for the moon to orbit the Earth once.

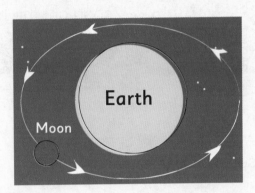

We can see the moon because it reflects light from the Sun.

1   **2**   **3**   **4**

1 The moon is in the shade of the Earth, so the moon appears dark.

2 Part of the moon is reflecting light, the rest is still shaded by the Earth.

3 As the moon moves through its orbit, it can reflect more light.

4 We can see the moon clearly as more light is reflected from its surface.

Wizard's Practice

Finish these sentences.

1 One rotation of the Earth takes _____ .

2 It takes _____ for the moon to orbit the Earth.

3 It takes _____ for the Earth to orbit the Sun.

4 All of the planets are _____ in shape.

5 The Earth is spinning all the time and we call this _____ .

Workbook page 32

Sound

Did you know that when objects vibrate they produce sound? Don't worry, you'll soon get the hang of it!

Vibrations

All sounds are caused by **vibrations**.

The vibrating object causes the air particles to vibrate. As the air particles vibrate they form invisible waves that carry the sound.

The larger the vibrations, the louder the sound. The harder you hit a drum, the louder the sound. Super!

We measure the volume of sound in **decibels**. A quiet sound will have a smaller number on the decibel scale.

 When a sound is made something is vibrating.

Hearing sound

We hear sounds because the vibrating air particles enter our ears. These vibrations pass through your ear and send a message to your brain.

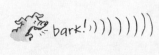 bark!)))))))))

Sounds travel through the air. Sounds have to travel through different materials before you can hear them. Sounds can travel through solids, liquids and gases. They travel best through solids. Sound travels through solids the easiest as there are more particles to carry the sound. Try putting your ear at one end of a bench whilst someone taps the other end of the bench. The sound is much louder than if you listen to the tapping through the air! The further away you are from the sound, the harder it is to hear.

 The symbol for decibels in dB. This will save you writing the word out lots of times.

Reducing sound

The closer you are to a noisy object, the louder you can hear it.

Loud sounds can damage your ears. People working in noisy places protect their ears with ear mufflers. Air is a good **insulator** of sound, because it does not let the sound pass through easily.

I would like to make some ear mufflers but I don't know which type of material to use. I have cotton wool, paper and bubble wrap.

I attach a sound sensor to a data logger. I wrap material around the sensor, then Wizard Whimstaff rings a bell and I record the sound levels.

To make this a fair test, I only change one factor. I am changing the type of material.

I keep these factors the same:

How hard we ring the bell.

The distance of the sound sensor from the bell.

The amount of material wrapped around the sensor.

My results show that the bubble wrap is best at insulating sound.
The key is the air. Materials are surrounded by air, but if the air is actually trapped inside the material, then that material is a better insulator.

 Air trapped inside ear mufflers insulates the ear from loud noises.

 MAGIC WORDS vibrations · decibels · insulator

Workbook page 33

Wizard's Practice

Match the word to its correct meaning.

1. vibrations   larger vibrations

2. louder   movement of materials or objects that causes sound

3. decibels   the unit used to measure sound levels

4. insulator   how loud or how quiet a sound is

5. volume   reduces the volume of sound

Music

Wizard Whimstaff is trying to teach me how to sing, but it is very difficult because all I can do is roar. There are lots of ways to make music though.

Musical instruments.

Sound is made when objects or materials **vibrate**. To make music from this guitar I need to pluck the strings. Plucking the strings makes them vibrate.

Wizard Whimstaff says that wind instruments make music differently. When Pointy blows into a recorder, the column of air vibrates and makes music.

I can play a drum though. When I hit the drum skin with my drumstick, the skin vibrates and makes a sound. The harder I hit the drum, the louder the sound.

Listening to very loud sounds can damage your ears.

Pitch

Some sounds seem very high and others seem low. Wizard Whimstaff says that this is called the **pitch**. I know a little girl that screams with a very high pitch!

My big drum makes a different sound so that must be a low pitch. My smaller drum makes a sound with a higher pitch. Wizard Whimstaff says the more material vibrating, the lower the pitch. Dabracababa! When I tighten the skin on my drum the pitch becomes higher.

This must be the same for guitar strings. Longer guitar strings have a lower pitch. By shortening the guitar string we can have a higher pitch.

Investigating pitch.

I am going to do an investigation to see if the amount of air affects the pitch. Wizard Whimstaff says that to make this a fair test I can only change one factor, so I will change the amount of air.

I can do this by putting different amounts of water into my bottles. I will then blow across the top of the bottles, which will make the air vibrate.

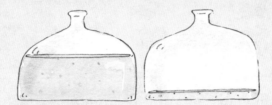

To make this a fair test I will keep these factors the same:

The type and size of bottle.

How hard I blow.

I found that the bottle with a lot of water made a higher note. The bottle with a little water made a lower note.

My conclusion is that the more air there is, the lower the pitch will be.

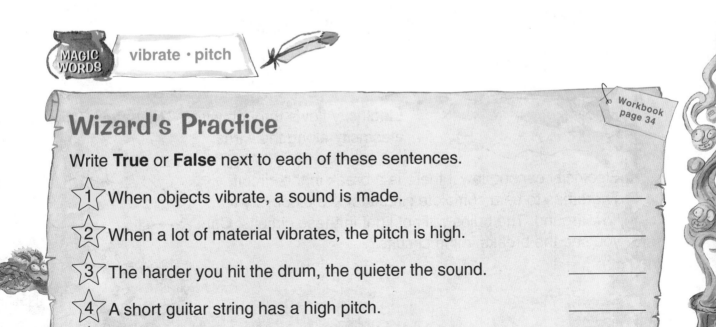

Workbook page 34

Wizard's Practice

Write **True** or **False** next to each of these sentences.

1. When objects vibrate, a sound is made. _____

2. When a lot of material vibrates, the pitch is high. _____

3. The harder you hit the drum, the quieter the sound. _____

4. A short guitar string has a high pitch. _____

5. To carry out a fair test, you should only change one factor. _____

Electric circuits

Electricity plays an important part in your everyday life. So let me tell you about how electricity moves around a circuit.

 Complete circuits.

Many toys and games use **electricity** from **batteries**.

Inside the battery, chemicals react together to generate electricity. You can buy different types of batteries to provide different amounts of electricity. More powerful batteries provide a greater voltage.

We use batteries to investigate electric circuits, because they are safer than the mains electricity. Electricity from the mains sockets is very dangerous and could kill you, so you should never:

Push things into an electric socket.

Play with electric plugs and sockets.

Touch plugs or switches with wet hands.

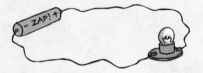

Electricity flows through wires. The battery forces the electricity along the wires.

Electricity cannot flow if there is a break in the circuit. There has to be a complete circuit for the electricity to flow around. The bulbs will not light in these circuits. Can you see the breaks in the circuits?

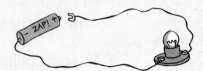

We use electricity at home for cooking, light, heat and television.

Circuit diagrams.

Now young wizard, when you draw a circuit diagram, you don't draw pictures of the different parts. You need to draw symbols instead. Allakazan! Here are some circuit symbols:

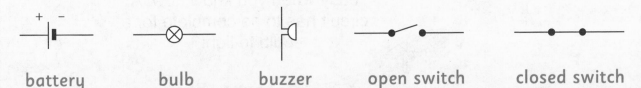

| battery | bulb | buzzer | open switch | closed switch |

You join the symbols with straight lines to represent the wires.

Conductors and insulators.

Let me tell you about electrical conductors. Materials that allow electricity to flow through them easily are called **conductors**.

Metals are good electrical conductors. The pins of a plug and the wires inside connecting flexes are made of metal to allow electricity to flow.

Some materials, like plastic, do not allow electricity to flow through them. These materials are called electrical **insulators**. This is why the outer case of a plug is made of plastic.

MAGIC WORDS electricity · conductors · insulators

Wizard's Practice

Workbook page 35

Underline the correct answer.

1. Batteries are used to provide   light   electricity   sound.

2. Electricity can only flow when the circuit is   hot   coloured   complete.

3. Materials that allow electricity to flow easily are called

   creators   conductors   insulators.

4. Materials that do not allow electricity to flow are called

   creators   conductors   insulators.

Brighter, faster

Making bulbs shine brighter is easy when you know how! A circuit has to be complete for a bulb to light.

⭐ Changing batteries.

We can make the bulbs in a circuit shine brighter by adding more batteries. Using less bulbs in the circuit will also make each bulb shine more brightly. Super!

These bulbs are in series. The electricity has to pass through each bulb in the circuit.

Now these bulbs are set up in parallel. The electricity is not shared between the bulbs, so they can shine more brightly than bulbs set up in series.

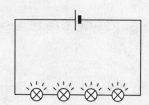

These changes can also make buzzers buzz louder and motors turn faster.

⭐ Faulty circuits.

Miss Snufflebeam has set up some circuits, but the bulbs will not light. Let's take a look at them to understand what is wrong.

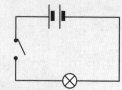

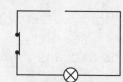

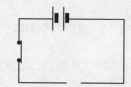

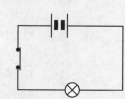

This one is easy! The switch has been left open, so the electricity cannot flow around the circuit.

Miss Snufflebeam has forgotten to put the battery in the circuit, so there is no electricity.

The bulb has been unscrewed, which causes a break in the circuit.

The batteries are facing each other, so the electricity cannot flow around the circuit.

Investigating wires.

I am carrying out an **investigation** to see if the length of a wire affects how brightly a bulb will shine. To make this a fair test I will only change one factor, the length of wire. I will keep all of the following factors the same:

Metal the wire is made from.   Thickness of the wire.

Size of bulb.   Size of battery.

Here are my results.

length of wire in cm	brightness of bulb
50	bright
100	dim glow
150	very faint
200	not lit

My conclusion is that the shorter the wire, the brighter the bulb.

The longer the wire, the further the electricity has to travel to get to the bulb.

MAGIC WORDS   investigation

Wizard's Practice

Workbook page 36

Finish these sentences.

1. We can make the bulbs brighter by adding more _____ to the circuit.

2. We can make buzzers louder by using a more powerful _____ .

3. Bulbs set up in parallel will be brighter than bulbs set up in _____ .

4. Bulbs will not light up if the _____ is left open.

5. To carry out a fair test you must only change one _____ and keep all the rest the same.

Forces

Brain cell alert! Forces are all around us. It is a force that pulls us back to the ground when we hop.

Different types of forces.

Croak! There are lots of different types of **forces**.

Some examples of forces are:

Push, pull, turn, twist.

Friction.

Gravity.

Air resistance.

Upthrust.

Magnetism.

Gravity is the force that pulls objects towards the Earth. Burp! When we jump, gravity pulls us back down.

The Earth is large with a large **mass**, and smaller objects are pulled towards it. This pull is the force of gravity. Our Earth is held in orbit around the Sun by the Sun's pull of gravity. The Sun is larger than the Earth.

Our moon is held in orbit around the Earth by the Earth's gravity. There is some gravity on the moon. However, because the moon is smaller than the Earth, there is less gravity on the moon.

 Without gravity, things would float away.

Measuring forces.

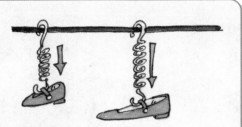

Slurp! We can measure force by using a forcemeter. The forcemeter measures the pull of gravity.

The unit of force is a **newton**. This is named after the famous scientist Sir Issac Newton.

We have **weight** because of gravity. Slurp! If we could send Pointy into space he would become weightless. This is because there would not be a large planet close by to give a pull of gravity.

If Pointy landed on the moon he would weigh less than he does on the Earth. This is because the moon is smaller than the Earth.

Stretching springs.

Croak! Inside the forcemeter is a spring. As you put objects on a spring, the downwards force stretches the spring.

When we take the objects off, the upwards force acting on the spring pulls it back into its original shape.

 MAGIC WORDS   force · gravity · mass · newton · weight

Workbook page 37

Wizard's Practice

Use the magic words to finish these sentences.

1. The force that pulls objects towards the Earth is called _____ .

2. Push, pull, twist, turn, friction and magnetism are all examples of _____ .

3. We can measure force with a _____ .

4. The pull of gravity pulling down on us is our _____ .

5. The unit of force is a _____ .

Slowing down

Now young wizard, I need to tell you about the forces that try to slow us down. **Friction** is the force caused when objects are pulled against each other. Rough surfaces have greater friction.

Friction

Friction is useful. It helps us to walk and it stops cars sliding around. Smooth surfaces have less friction. When there is snow and ice on the ground we have less friction, so we slip and slide.

When it snows, we lay salt and grit on the roads, so that vehicles slide less on the slippery ice. Also, shoes have grips and grooves on the bottom, so that we don't slip and fall over.

Air resistance.

When I fly on my broomstick, **air resistance** slows me down.

Air resistance is a useful force when it acts against a parachute. It slows the parachute down so that the person can land safely. Hey presto!

You use air resistance when you fly a kite.

Water resistance.

Mugly and Bugly can move through the water easily, but **water resistance** slows them down. Their curved shape helps to reduce the water resistance acting upon them.

Boats move easily through the water. They are built with a shape that reduces water resistance. Some shapes slow an object down.

I am carrying out an investigation to see which shapes move most easily through water. I am making this a fair test by only changing one factor. The factor I am changing is the shape. I use a piece of plasticine™ and mould it into different shapes. I drop my plasticine™ shape into a bottle of water and time how long it takes to fall to the bottom.

To ensure that this is a fair test I keep these factors the same:

Piece of plasticine™.   Amount of water.

Bottle of water.   Dropping plasticine™ shape
                               from the same height.

My conclusion is that the smooth, narrow objects fell to the bottom quicker, because they reduced the amount of water resistance.

 MAGIC WORDS   friction · air resistance · water resistance

Wizard's Practice

Workbook page 38

Circle the correct word in each sentence.

 When two objects pull against each other, they create a force of
   freezing / friction .

 When we have snow and ice on the ground, the force of friction is
   greater / smaller .

More friction is provided by surfaces that are smooth / rough .

 Mugly and Bugly are the correct shape to reduce

   water retention / water resistance .

 Air resistance is useful to a parachute / rocket .

Balanced and unbalanced forces

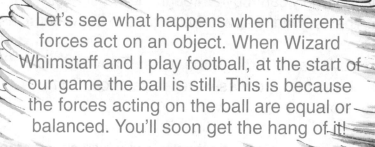

Let's see what happens when different forces act on an object. When Wizard Whimstaff and I play football, at the start of our game the ball is still. This is because the forces acting on the ball are equal or balanced. You'll soon get the hang of it!

⭐ Balanced forces.

Several forces act upon objects all the time. The pull of **gravity** on a football is equal to the **upthrust** from the ground, so the ball is still.

When balanced forces act upon a moving object, the object will continue to move in the same direction at the same speed.

 When objects are still, we sometimes say they are stationary.

⭐ Unbalanced forces.

Miss Snufflebeam kicks the ball and it moves. Super! The force from the kick means that the forces are now unbalanced.

As the ball moves across the grass, **friction** is acting upon it. The forces are unbalanced and the ball will come to a stop. Then the forces are balanced again.

 Unbalanced forces change the speed or direction of movement of an object.

Force diagrams.

To help us understand the effect of forces, we draw arrows onto pictures to show the forces. The direction of the force can be shown by the arrow head. The size of the arrow represents the size of the force. When our football is still, all of the forces acting upon it are equal or balanced.

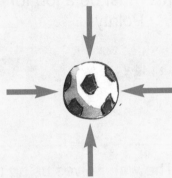

This **force diagram** shows what happens when Wizard Whimstaff kicks the ball.

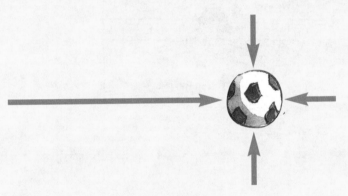

The football is moving because the forces are unbalanced.

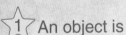

Workbook page 39

Wizard's Practice

Write **True** or **False** for each sentence.

 1 An object is still because the forces are balanced. _____

2 An object keeps moving in the same direction and at the same speed because the forces are balanced. _____

 3 The car is accelerating so the forces must be balanced. _____

 4 Gravity and upthrust are never balanced. _____

5 The car is slowing down because the forces are unbalanced. _____

Floating and sinking

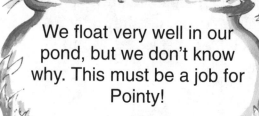

We float very well in our pond, but we don't know why. This must be a job for Pointy!

Floating

Croak! We float in water. The water gives us an upwards force. This force is called an **upthrust**. This upthrust balances our weight, so we can float.

All objects experience an upthrust in water.

Sinking

When you go swimming, the water gives you an upwards force. This force is called an upthrust. This upthrust balances your weight, so you can float.

When you jump into a swimming pool, you have to dive into the water so that you can sink. You make your body narrow. This means there is less upthrust acting upon you, so your weight is the greater force. The forces are unbalanced, so you sink.

To move deeper down into the pool, you have to kick with your back legs. This push on the water moves you forwards. This forwards force is called thrust. When you stop kicking, the upthrust becomes the greater force and so you float to the surface.

Investigating boats.

Brain cell alert! We are investigating boats. Mugly wants to know why boats float. When we drop a pebble into our pond it sinks. We think it sinks because it is heavy, but we are heavier than the pebble and we can float. Boats are very heavy and they can float.

Wizard Whimstaff says that it is all about the surface area of the object.

In our investigation we have two pieces of metal foil. We squeeze one piece of foil into a small ball. We leave the other flat. We will try to float both pieces of metal foil on the surface of water.

The flat piece of metal foil floats, but the ball of metal sinks.

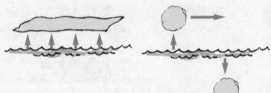

The flat piece of foil gives a greater surface area, so more upthrust can act upon the metal.

The forces are balanced, so the metal floats.

Wizard's Practice

Workbook page 40

Finish these sentences.

1. When Mugly and Bugly swim through water, their back legs provide _____ .

2. All objects in water have a force pushing up on them, which is called _____ .

3. When forces are balanced, objects will _____ .

4. The area of the surface of an object is called its _____ .

5. When the weight of the object is greater than the upthrust, the object will _____ .

Wizard's Challenge

 Magnets

Croak! We like to play with magnets. We use a magnet to find iron nails.

a What other objects would our magnet attract? Tick the box.

plastic spoon ☐   steel paper clip ☐

Pointy's wooden wand ☐   Wizard Whimstaff's cloak ☐

b When we hold our magnets next to each other they are **attracted** together. Write **N** or **S** on the magnet to show their poles.

c Bugly turns one of the magnets around. As we place them to each other the other magnet moves away. Explain why.

_____

2 Shadows

a A tree casts a shadow across our garden. This is because the tree is…
Finish the sentence by circling the correct answer.

opaque   solid   wood

b At what time of day will a shadow be shortest? Tick the correct box.

10:00 am ☐   12:00 midday ☐   6:00 pm ☐

c During the day the Sun appears to move across the sky.

Explain why.

_____

_____

3 Earth, Sun and moon.

The moon does not give out light. It reflects light from the Sun.

a Which sentence explains how we know that the moon does not give out light? Tick the correct box.

The moon changes position in the sky. ☐

The moon is a sphere but it appears to change shape. ☐

We can only see the moon at night. ☐

b Draw **two** arrows on the diagram to show how the person can see the moon.

4 Electric circuits.

Burp! Pointy is setting up electric circuits. He has set up a battery, a bulb and two wires.

Pointy puts different objects in the circuit to see which ones will allow the bulb to light up. Below is his results table.

a Draw one tick for each object. We have done the first one for you.

object	bulb lights up	bulb does not light up
plastic comb		✔
steel spoon		
paper cup		
wooden wand		
metal scissors		

SATs Practice

Award 1 mark
for each box p[?]
correct answe[?]

1 a Draw lines to match each food group to its use in the body.

| growth and repair | extra energy if needed and to keep us warm | energy for playing and running |

☐
☐
☐

b Which of the following sentences best describes a healthy diet? Tick the correct box.

Eating lots of chips. ☐

Eating a small amount of each type of food. ☐

Not eating chocolate. ☐

Eating only fresh fruit. ☐

☐

2 Seeds need to move away from the plant. This is called dispersal. Draw lines to match each picture to a label.

| animal or bird dispersal | explosion dispersal | wind dispersal |

☐
☐
☐

3 Camels are adapted to their habitat.

a Circle the habitat for a camel.

desert   forest   sea

b Draw three lines to match each adaptation with how it helps the camel to survive.

wide, flat feet   to protect eyes from strong sunlight

leathery eyelids   to store food and water

fleshy hump on back   to stop them sinking into the sand

c Describe one way in which a fish is adapted for its habitat.

_____

_____

4 Mugly and Bugly watched the caterpillars eating the lettuce plants. A bird flew down and ate a caterpillar, then the cat jumped out of the hedge and ate the bird.

a Use this information to finish the food chain.

lettuce ➞ ( ) ➞ ( ) ➞ ( )

b Put **one** tick in each row to describe each part of the food chain. The first one has been done for you.

part of food chain	producer	predator	prey	predator and prey
lettuce	✓			
bird				
caterpillar				
cat				

c Why is the lettuce a producer?

_____

5 Mugly and Bugly are playing with some objects.

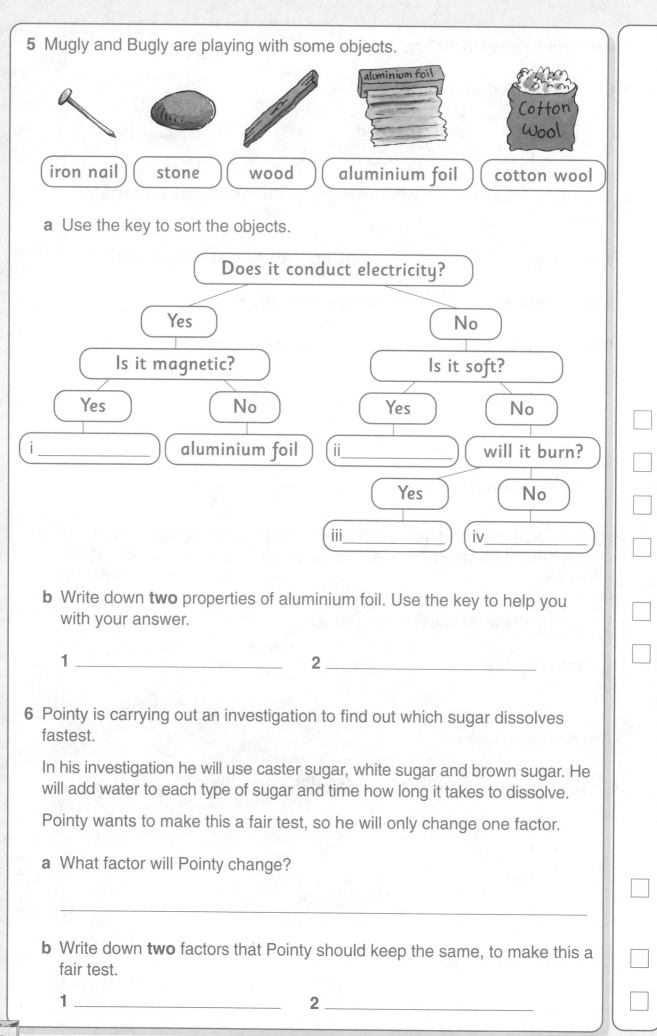

iron nail | stone | wood | aluminium foil | cotton wool

a Use the key to sort the objects.

Does it conduct electricity?

Yes | No

Is it magnetic? | Is it soft?

Yes | No | Yes | No

i _____ | aluminium foil | ii_____ | will it burn?

Yes | No

iii_____ | iv_____

b Write down **two** properties of aluminium foil. Use the key to help you with your answer.

1 _____   2 _____

6 Pointy is carrying out an investigation to find out which sugar dissolves fastest.

In his investigation he will use caster sugar, white sugar and brown sugar. He will add water to each type of sugar and time how long it takes to dissolve.

Pointy wants to make this a fair test, so he will only change one factor.

a What factor will Pointy change?

_____

b Write down **two** factors that Pointy should keep the same, to make this a fair test.

1 _____   2 _____

Here are Pointy's results.

c Draw a bar chart of Pointy's results.

type of sugar	time taken to dissolve in mins
caster sugar	10
white sugar	25
brown sugar	45

(bar chart: y-axis "time taken to dissolve in mins" marked 0 to 50 in 5s; x-axis "type of sugar" with caster sugar, white sugar, brown sugar)

d Explain how Pointy will know that the sugar has dissolved.

7 Wizard Whimstaff is playing drums.

a Wizard Whimstaff hits the drum harder with his stick. What happens to the sound? Circle the correct word.

louder   quieter   high pitch   low pitch

b Pointy walks away from Wizard Whimstaff. What happens to the loudness of the sound that Pointy hears as he walks away? Circle the correct word.

louder   quieter   high pitch   low pitch

c Wizard Whimstaff tightens the drum skin. How does this affect the sound?

louder   quieter   higher pitch   lower pitch

d Describe what happens to the drum skin to make the sound.

How did you do?

0–15 Fair attempt, but more practice needed!

16–23 Good try, you are getting there!

24–30 Well done, a super science score!

31–36 You are as clever as Wizard Whimstaff!

Answers

Page 5
Food
1 bread and pasta — growth and repair
2 meat and cheese — energy to play and run
3 fruit and vegetables — extra energy
4 butter and crisps — help us to digest our food

Page 7
Teeth
1 incisors
2 molars
3 sweets or sugary foods
4 dentist
5 canines

Page 9
Skeleton and movement
1 supports
2 strong
3 outside
4 muscles
5 pairs

Page 11
Heart and blood
1 ribs
2 arteries
3 increases
4 70 beats per minute

Page 13
Growing up
1 T
2 F
3 F
4 T
5 T

Page 14-15
Wizard's Challenge
1 a group 1
  carbohydrates provide energy
  b group 3
  any one from:
  to keep us healthy; to give us vitamins, minerals, fibre; to help us digest food
2 a molars
  b any two from:
  brush teeth twice a day
  avoid sugary foods
  visit dentist regularly
  use floss and mouth wash
3 a

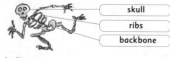

skull
ribs
backbone

  b skull
  c Muscles work in pairs, one pulls whilst the other relaxes.
4 a The heart pumps blood around the body at a faster rate.
  b Pulse rate increases and then decreases again after he has stopped.
5 take plenty of exercise
  drink lots of water
  eat a balanced diet

Page 17
Growing plants
1 warmth, water
2 leaves
3 roots
4 germination
5 wilt

Page 19
Plants make their own food
1 leaves
2 water
3 sunlight
4 producers
5 leaves

Page 21
Flowering plant
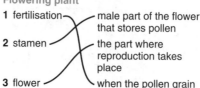
1 fertilisation — male part of the flower that stores pollen
2 stamen — the part where reproduction takes place
3 flower — when the pollen grain fuses with the egg
4 ovary — formed after fertilisation, will develop into new plants
5 seeds — female part of the flower where the ovum is stored

Page 23
Life cycle of plants
1 seed dispersal
2 fertilisation
3 wind, insects (any order)
4 any two from: air, water, light, shelter
5 seeds

Pages 24-25
Wizard's Challenge
1 a temperature
  b any two from:
  number of seeds
  type of seeds
  type of tub
  amount of water
  time seeds left for
  c So it is a fair test.
  d Seeds germinate best in warm temperatures.
2 a air, light, water
  b leaf
3 a

stigma   stamen
petal   ovary
style   sepal

  b stamen (accept anther)
  c sepal
4 a pollination, seed dispersal
  b Germination is when a seed develops into a small plant.

Page 27
Habitats
1 False
2 True
3 False
4 False
5 True

Page 29
Identification
1 invertebrates — parts of an animal or plant used to identify them
2 vertebrates — animals without backbones
3 features — animals with backbones
4 classification key — a way of sorting animals and plants into groups
5 Venn diagram — a method of identifying animals and plants

Page 31
Food chains
1 T
2 F
3 T
4 F
5 T

Page 33
Soil and rocks
1 particles
2 rocks
3 soil
4 fertiliser
5 nutrients

Page 35
Harmful microbes
1 bacteria, fungi
2 life processes
3 food poisoning, ear infections
4 microbes (accept fungi)
5 plaque

Page 37
Helpful microbes
1 bread
2 paper
3 warmth
4 decay
5 penicillin

Pages 38-39
Wizard's Challenge
1 a

  b A place where animals and plants live.
2 a animal A = squirrel
  animal B = butterfly
  animal C = bird
  animal D = slug
3 a grass → rabbit → fox
  b There would be more rabbits.
  (accept: with less rabbits there would be more grass)
4 a sandy soil B, clay soil A
  b More water drained through the sandy soil.
  or
  Less water drained through the clay soil.
5 a any one from:
  wine, beer, bread, cheese, yoghurt
  b viruses

Page 41
Properties of materials
1 window — material that can be polished and made reflective
2 mirror — material that is soft and insulates heat
3 saucepan — material that is transparent
4 coat — material that is hard and can be sharpened
5 knife — material that conducts heat.

Page 43
Solids and liquids
1 False
2 True
3 True
4 False
5 True

Page 45
Gases
1 air — a gas used inside balloons to make them rise
2 carbon dioxide — the gas I breathe in and use inside my body
3 helium — a mixture of gases that is all around us
4 oxygen — has mass, can flow easily and fills a container
5 properties of air — a gas used to make drinks fizzy

Page 47
Changing state
1 evaporation (accept evaporating)
2 condensing (accept condensation)
3 solid
4 liquid
5 water cycle

Page 49
Dissolving
1 F
2 F
3 T
4 T
5 F

Page 51
Separating mixtures
1 magnetism
2 a sieve
3 filter paper

Page 53
Reversible changes
1 reversible
2 distillation
3 evaporation, condensation
4 dissolve
5 filter

Page 55
Irreversible changes
1 R
2 I
3 R
4 I
5 R

Page 57
Temperature change
1 thermometer — material that will not allow heat to flow through
2 temperature — material that allows heat to flow through easily
3 insulator — an instrument to measure temperature
4 thermal conductor — a measure of how hot or how cold something is
5 degrees Celcius — unit of temperature

Page 59
Keeping Warm
1 False
2 True
3 True
4 False
5 True

Pages 60-61
Wizard's Challenge
1 conducts heat
2

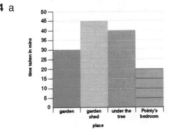

gas
liquid
solid

3 a sieve
  b filter the mixture (to remove sand)
    evaporate salt water (to remove water)
4 a

  b Pointy's bedroom
5 a any one from:
    same size cup
    same shape of cup
    same starting temperature of coffee
    same volume of coffee
    left in the same room
    left for the same amount of time
  b Cup A kept the coffee warmer for the longer time.
    or
    The coffee cooled more quickly in cup B.

Page 63
Magnets
1 R 2 A 3 R 4 N 5 A

Page 65
Seeing the light
1 straight lines
2 reflection
3 ray diagram
4 metal foil
5 the Sun

Page 67
Shadows
1 T
2 F
3 T
4 F
5 T

Page 69
Earth, Sun and moon
1 24 hours
2 28 days
3 one year (365 years)
4 spherical
5 rotation

Page 71
Sound
1 vibrations — larger vibrations
2 louder — movement of materials or objects that causes sound
3 decibels — the unit used to measure sound levels
4 insulator — how loud or how quiet a sound is
5 volume — reduces the volume of sound

Page 73
Music
1 True
2 False
3 False
4 True
5 True

Page 75
Electric circuits
1 electricity
2 complete
3 conductors
4 insulators

Page 77
Brighter, faster
1 batteries
2 battery
3 series
4 switch
5 factor

Page 79
Forces
1 gravity
2 forces
3 forcemeter
4 weight
5 newton

Page 81
Slowing down
1 friction
2 smaller
3 rough
4 water resistance
5 parachute

Page 83
Balanced and unbalanced forces
1 True
2 True
3 False
4 False
5 True

Page 85
Floating and sinking
1 thrust   4 surface area
2 upthrust   5 sink
3 float

Pages 86-87
Wizard's Challenge
1 a steel paper clip
  b The magnets should be labelled so that N and S are facing each other.
  c The magnet is being repelled.
    or
    The facing poles are the same.

2 a opaque
  b 12:00 midday
  b The Earth rotates every 24 hours.

3 a The moon is a sphere but it appears to change shape.
  b

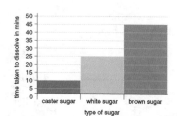

4 a

objects	bulb lights up	bulb does not light up
plastic comb		✓
steel spoon	✓	
paper cup		✓
wooden wand		✓
metal scissors	✓	

Pages 88-91
SATs Practice
1 a

  b Eating a small amount of each type of food.

2

3 a desert
  b

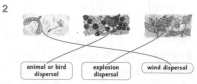

    wide, flat feet — to protect eyes from strong sunlight
    leathery eyelids — to store food and water
    fleshy hump on back — to stop them sinking into the sand

---

c Any one from: gills to help it breathe, scales for protection, fins for steering and balance, coloured for camouflage

4 a lettuce → caterpillar → bird → cat
  b

part of food chain	producer	predator	prey	predator and prey
lettuce	✓			
bird				✓
caterpillar			✓	
cat		✓		

  c Lettuce is a green plant so it is able to produce its own food using light from the sun and a green chemical found inside its leaves.

5 a i   iron nail
    ii   cotton wool
    iii   wood
    iv   stone
  b conducts electricity, not magnetic

6 a type of sugar
  b any two from: the volume of water, the temperature of the water, the amount of sugar, the container that is used
  c

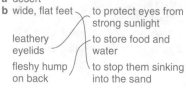

  d The sugar will no longer be visible and the water will be clear.

7 a louder
  b quieter
  c higher pitch
  d The skin vibrates and makes a sound.

Glossary

adapted plants and animals adapt to their habitat by developing features that help them to survive

air resistance the force that slows objects down as they move through the air

arteries blood vessels that carry blood away from your heart

bacteria microbes that can cause illnesses such as food poisoning and ear infections, although some bacteria are helpful and can be used in food production

blood liquid that is moving around your body all the time, carrying food and oxygen to all parts of your body

blood vessels small tubes that carry blood around your body

canines cone shaped teeth at the side of your mouth, used for tearing food

carbohydrates are found in foods like pasta, potatoes and bread. Your body uses them for energy

carbon dioxide a gas in the air that is used in fire extinguishers and to make drinks fizzy

carnivore an animal that eats other animals

circuit when wires and electrical parts are joined in a continuous loop

community all the living things in a habitat

conclusion what you have learnt from your investigation

condensation when a gas changes into a liquid

conductors materials that allow electricity to flow through them easily

decay when microbes feed on materials to break them down

decibels(db) units used to measure sound levels

digest the breaking down of food

dissolving when solids break down and move into the spaces between water particles, forming a clear solution

distillation method of separating a mixture of two liquids by using evaporation and condensation

ecosystem a habitat and its community

electrical circuit components joined by wires to allow electricity to flow around a complete circuit

electricity a type of energy that flows through wires

evaporation when a liquid changes into a gas

excretion going to the toilet

factor something that can be changed

fair test when only one factor is changed and all others are kept the same, so you can be sure of knowing what caused your results

fats found in foods like butter. It helps to insulate your body and can be used for extra energy

features parts of a plant or animal, such as shape of leaf or number of legs

fertilisation when a pollen grain fuses with an egg

fertiliser animal droppings or chemicals, which are added to soil to improve its condition

fibre found in fruit and vegetables. It helps us to digest our food

filter when filter paper is used to separate smaller solid particles from a liquid

food chain way of showing who eats what

food web several food chains linked together

force type of energy that changes the speed and direction of an object

force diagram simple diagram showing lines of force acting on an object

freeze when a liquid changes to a solid

friction the force caused when objects are pulled against each other

fungi can be microbes or larger plants, such as mushrooms. Fungi cannot produce their own food in the same way as green plants

gas particles are spread apart so they can flow more easily than liquids. They fill the container they are in, do not keep their shape and can be squashed into a smaller space

germination when seeds develop into tiny plants

gravity a force that pulls smaller objects towards larger objects, e.g. all objects are pulled towards the Earth

habitat place where animals and plants live

heart the organ that pumps blood around your body

herbivore animal that eats plants

incisors teeth at the front of your mouth with a sharp cutting edge, which are used to bite your food

insoluble materials that can still be seen when they are added to water, because they do not dissolve

insulators materials that do not allow electricity to flow through them

invertebrates animals without a backbone

investigation to carefully examine something

irreversible a change that cannot be put back to how it was at the start e.g. boiling an egg

joint where two or more bones meet, allowing movement to take place

life cycle stages a living thing passes through during its life

liquid has particles that are further apart than in a solid, so they flow easily and take the shape of their container

magnetic a metal that is attracted to a magnet is magnetic. A metal that is not attracted to a magnet is non-magnetic

mass amount of material in an object

material what all things are made of

melt when a solid changes to a liquid

micro-organisms (or microbes) tiny, living things which are so small you need a microscope to see them. Includes bacteria, viruses and some fungi

molars teeth at the back of your mouth, which are wider and flatter on the top and used for chewing food

Mrs Gren to help you remember the seven life processes: **m**oving, **r**eproduction, **s**ensitivity, **g**rowth, **r**espiration, **e**xcretion and **n**utrition

muscles attached to bones to allow the bones to move

newton unit of force, named after the famous scientist Sir Issac Newton

nutrients simple chemicals absorbed into the blood of animals or through the roots in plants. Used by the body for growth and movement

ovum egg cell

ovary female part of the flower where eggs are stored

oxygen gas in the air, which we breath in. It combines with the food we eat to give us energy

particles tiny pieces of matter that all things are made of

pitch how high or low a sound can be heard. More material vibrating causes a lower pitch

plaque a sticky substance found on your teeth, which is made by bacteria as they feed on the sugars left in your mouth. Plaque causes teeth to decay

pollen male part of a plant

pollination when pollen is moved from one flower to another by wind or insects

producers green plants that produce their own food. They are usually the start of a food chain

properties characteristics of materials, such as flexible, conducts electricity, magnetic etc.

protein found in foods like meat and fish. It helps your body to grow bigger and stronger

pulse when your heart pumps, the blood is forced through your arteries. This causes a ripple through your arteries, which is called a pulse

ray diagram diagram using straight lines and arrow heads to show the direction in which light travels

reproduction when living things produce offspring

reversible change that we can change back to how it was at the start e.g. ice melting

saturated solution all of the spaces between the water particles become full, so no more solid can dissolve

seed dispersal when seeds are moved away from the parent plant, by animals, wind, explosion or water

skeleton the collection of bones inside your body, which supports and holds you upright

solid has particles close together, so they do not change shape easily and do not flow. Some can conduct heat and electricity

soluble materials that dissolve to form a clear solution

solution when soluble materials dissolve in a liquid

stamen male part of the flower where pollen is stored

states of matter solid, liquid and gas are the three states of matter

stigma female part of a flower, which has a sticky upper surface where pollen lands

style the narrow tube in a flower joining the stigma to the ovary

temperature measure of how hot or how cold something is, usually in degrees Celsius

thermal conductor a material that allows heat to pass through it easily

thermal insulator a material that does not allow heat to pass through it easily

upthrust upwards force

veins blood vessels that carry blood back to the heart

Venn diagram a diagram made from two circles, grouping or classifying items according to the characteristics they share

vertebrates animals with backbones

vibrations moving rapidly back and forth

viruses microbes that can cause illnesses, such as flu and measles

water cycle shows how water changes state naturally

water resistance force that slows objects down as they move through water

water vapour water particles in the air, such as steam

weight measure of the pull of gravity on an object

wilt when plants do not have enough water they go floppy, which is known as wilting

yeast microbe used to make bread, wine and beer